Heritage – The Family

My inspiration for writing this account of my life came from an excerpt of my Great Great Grandfathers diary written in 1826. One of the most significant entries for me was the declaration he made when sixteen years of age. He declared total abstinence from alcohol and also recorded some sixty years later that he had held fast to his temperance. That is truly amazing to me as it took 25 years of pain and depravation to drive me to such a decision.

However as I celebrate the arrival of my twenty sixth year of sobriety in 2014, I have a lot to be grateful for and I do it with sense of pride as it has been a difficult journey. I have mourned the passing of my Mother, Muriel in 1996 and the termination of two marriages which quite frankly is much more complex to overcome than the passing of a loved one as these individuals are still around constantly reminding me of my inability to manage long lasting relationships.

There is an upside to this defect of character endured by my ex longsuffering partners, in that I enjoy the privilege of having two beautiful daughters, Jennifer and Alisha, one handsome son, Jonathan and two gorgeous grandchildren, Jessica and Alastair.

I also look back on the relationships I had with various other women with great affection and the possibility that the Biggs seed may have flourished in other unknown heritage lines.

I have written about my parents in brief only as I saw them which is maybe not who they really were, but as I knew them to be.

I was also keen to try to describe how I see my children as my offspring are the most precious gift their Mothers could have given me. There are many amends I owe my children. I hope when I have had the opportunity in the past twenty five years of recovery that I have made a positive difference in their lives.

Great Grandfather Hugh Burden

Bewildered, Battered and Bruised
The Early Years
ONE

Muriel lay with her legs wide open. She had done it before and who knows maybe not for the last time either. Donald, her husband, was at work. It wasn't a secret and Donald had known about his wife's activities over the past months. Nine months before this episode he had himself been a naughty boy. He had spent a night of gratuitous sex and debauchery and the result led to Muriel's present predicament.

'Oh! I wish the wee bug would hurry up I'm starving', said Muriel. She was always very down to earth with her priorities well sussed out. Hunger was not an option, and it had become tiresome carrying me about for the last nine months. In those days it was not yet culturally acceptable to be present at the birth of your son. Dad was a man. Men didn't do such things, it was better to be at work and let the ladies do ladies things! So he was going to be absent from the arrival of his new born son.

It was the 14th of APRIL 1950 and the time was 5pm, time for tea in the hospital, and you ate at the allotted time or not at all, and that was not going to happen to Muriel, my Mother, in the outside world. We of course had been very close for the trimesters preceding this event.

One big push, and tea time. I of course obliged, I was to be a persistent 'people pleaser' from the outset! A good characteristic for an Alcoholic in the making.

Of course there were no cries of 'Oh, quick, put it back, it's an Alcoholic'. No, nobody knew what had entered the world. It was all tears of joy and hallelujahs. I cannot imagine what people would do if they anticipated the shear pain of living with an Alcoholic, or the years of frustration in the future with everyone concerned wondering what the hell was going on, especially the Alcoholic themselves.

So here was Arthur in all my glory, nude, screaming for food, and demanding love attention and understanding from the start. Not much changed in the coming years!

I already had a sister, Hilary who had popped out of Mum nearly three years before my arrival. Yes, it was not the first time my Daddy had been promiscuous with my Mummy, naughty boy. Now I do not want to make my sister out to be a psychopathic bully but ….. yes, I do.

Right, time to get my own back and put her indiscretions into print, so here goes, sorry Hilly, it just has to be done.

I was a cute wee bairn with blond curly hair, for a while anyway, that is, until my sister reached snapping point. Oh, how My Mum loved to hear the people say 'isn't he cute and look at his gorgeous curly hair'.

So, at the age of five, my sister was on look out duty for my Mum while she put the washing through the Mangle, a very old fashion way of tumble drying the clothes, then hung them out on the washing line in the back garden. On her return my Mum was greeted by a big smiley daughter and a very bald Son. I wasn't upset, my big sister had told me what a great idea it would be and how Mummy would love the new look.

Two years old and bald again, a pattern which was to be repeated throughout my life. A shiny new start for me. My hair grew back but this time in glorious Technicolor, red, GINGER no less. If I hadn't got enough troubles being a prospective Alcoholic, now I was also destined for the classic personal attention of every bully in the world who seems to think Gingerism is an invitation to tantalise and persecute our endangered species.

When Hilary was fifteen and I was twelve we had another of our clashes but this time I was bigger and prepared to defend my realm (King Arthur), as never before, and there had been one or two issues before. I was watching the TV on this particular Saturday afternoon. The wrestling, not sure who was fighting, maybe a tag match with the Eagle brothers, my favourites, or Big Daddy, another of my heroes. I had so many heroes in my head, Robin Hood, William Tell etc.. I always felt better about myself when I fantasized about being other people. Grandiosity, another great quality of the addictive personality,. There I go again, lost in wonderland, so back to the story.

 I was lost in paradise watching wrestling techniques, which were being stored for my next fight at school. 'Be prepared' the Scouts were teaching me, so I took it to heart.

 Off went the TV,' oh my God you can't do that' I screamed at my sister.

 ' I don't want to watch that so it's going off', she said proud as punch.

 'Bollocks to that it's going back on' I said, which it did. ON, off, on, off, on, off. Right, grappling time, and physical contact ensued between my sister and me. I was doing quite well, generally the arm locks and neck strangles were going fine, until I felt a powerful grasp on the back of my head which pulled me backward and then propelled my head forward to meet the oncoming skull of my sister. My Mother had very powerful arms from all the domestic work, not to mention the tennis and golf every week to keep her fit. We were stunned into submission with an ultimatum from the Matriarch. It was our last physical fight we had until we grew up and got married to our respective partners. From then on it was more hugs and caring between Brother and Sister. You may notice the capital S in Sister has arrived; I had dealt with my resentments toward Hilary from this point onward.

Hilary is a great person, very hard working , genuine and honest, extremely caring to all her family and one of the most determined people I have ever encountered, excepting my Mother.

 Hilary is a doer , and will tackle anything that comes her way. I think on reflection we made each other fairly tough as neither of us would ever back down, so now, in union, we are quite formidable. She was not afflicted with the Alcoholic genes passed down from my Grandpa Robertson, who died a heavy whisky drinker, Alcoholic? I don't know, but he couldn't stop when his family begged him for his sobriety.

He made a fortune then lost it through various dodgy deals, not illegal, just misguided. He was a lawyer in Edinburgh and a Grand Master of the Lodge. He made the money back but he also lost his 21 year old daughter, My Godmother, Roberta, to a slow and progressive Multiple Sclerosis. I think it was very hard to witness and it may have had significant influence on my Grandfather's spiritual wellbeing. Maybe he searched for his peace at the bottom of a bottle of whisky. The incident with the hair, which quite honestly I do not recall more than I have been told by both Mother and Sister, is an illustration of our initial relationship and how careful parents need to be when siblings are relating to situations around them even at an early age.

TWO

Trauma plays a significant role in my life. You need to know about the traumas as these play an important role in identifying my characteristics.

I can remember all of them vividly and they visit my consciousness every day resulting in a full blown illness at the age of fifty six. Starting with my own trauma, and later, from being witness to serious unnatural episodes involving other people.

I developed Post Traumatic Stress Disorder known as PTSD, which played a significant part in the collapse of my second marriage.

The personal incidents involved my head mainly, although there were one or two other parts that suffered through the attentions of adversaries amusing themselves at my expense. The first I remember was when I was about seven years old.

I had a desire to be good at all games, and there was one called 'Knifey'. This game required the precision throwing of a knife into the ground. It began with an opponent standing with his legs together.

You threw the knife to either side of the opponent's feet. The knife had to stick in the ground or it didn't count. If it did stick, then the opponent had to open his legs to the edge of the knife imbedded in the ground. It would get wider and wider as you might imagine so the final winning throw would be placed in the middle of the other guys legs.

This is the dangerous part and can be dependent on the opponents will to win, or alternatively, the temptation to injure the other by miss-throwing the knife around the other player's private parts. Enough about the game let's get back to the practice.

I could not find a knife so in my wisdom, and full of ingenuity I borrowed my Dad's Bradawl. This is a long pointy thing for making holes in wood.

I was doing well against myself. One to the left and one to the right, legs further and further apart, until I threw the one which turned out to be the last one of the day, as I imbedded it in my knee and through the Patella (knee bone as I found out much later in life). I am not sure if you have ever tried not to scream when the naughty prank went wrong.

I had been told in no uncertain terms not to mess with my Dad'stools as they were dangerous.

I did reach a conclusion that day, that sometimes my Dad was right.

Taking the Bradawl out of my knee proved more of a problem than you might think as bone is not forgiving, nor willing, to give up an intruder very easily. I summoned the courage from fear of retribution from my Father I think, and pulled the implement from the said Patella and spent the next half an hour thinking up an excuse for the wrongdoing in order to avoid the wrath of my Dad. Also practicing walking without a limp to avoid attention and any misplaced sympathy from my Mother.

This point is important and identifies my introduction to lying in order to avoid persecution, retribution or punishment. All of which I feared. Guilt and fear were always a significant reason for my need to cover up rather than be honest.

There have been several other cerebral traumas in my life involving my methods of transport, a tricycle, a bike, a Hillman Imp sport and a sledge.

I am very competitive, and this can be both an asset and a hindrance, depending on how you handle your level of commitment.

I used to time myself doing everything. If it wasn't fast enough I would try and try again. That was the problem with the Tricycle incident. I wanted to see how fast I could go down the hospital hill, which was adjacent to our house, in the Astley Ainsly hospital grounds.

A boiler room and massive chimney were at the bottom of the hill. It was a great place to play with tall oak trees full of conkers, and long grass to hide in. Also there was a sizable heap of coal for the furnaces. We played on that heap many a time with our swords made of wood and bows made from branches cut off the ewe tree, armed with garden canes for arrows with bird feather for flights. God, we were dangerous, Robin Hood, William Tell, King of the castle, defending the injustices of the world in a fantasy game between friends.

The road in which we lived was a cul-de-sac. Very safe with little traffic, and sloped from top to bottom, which in the winter became the 'Cresta Run' for our sledges. The sledges were hand made by ourselves or by my Dad. He was a genius at building things from wood and metal just like his Dad Arthur. Can you spot where I got the name? There were loads of kids in the street of all ages, so we were never short of friends to play with.

Even still I could entertain myself for hours on end, deep in my fantasy world. That did not change over the next few years, thirty years actually, I never grew up.

Here is a sweeping statement which I believe to be true, backed up by the entire female human race. 'Males do not mature until they are forty, if ever!' Well, I didn't at least. Have I told the tale of the Trike? No, I wandered again, so here goes.

THREE

First of all before I start, you may be asking yourself what is a 'trike'. Short for tricycle actually and it was my second one. I have a picture of me when I was two on an all metal three wheeler with solid rubber tyres, a metal seat and definitely no brakes. That was the first one. And the second was just a bigger version on the first, but this one had a chain drive instead of two pedals either side of the front wheel. Lots faster and I could do two wheel trick driving as it had a proper padded seat.

There was a fantastic track starting at the top of the hill adjacent to the hospital building, which meandered between the trees all the way to the boiler house at the bottom. The autumn leaves had fallen, giving off that dusky perfume indicating the coming of winter. The track was intended for the patients to enjoy the fresh air and greenery, ideal for rehabilitation, as long as there are no tricycles hurtling down at break neck speed, artfully guided by a six year old equivalent of Stirling Moss, the famous racing driver of the time and another of my fantasy heroes.

The poor old guy didn't know what didn't hit him. I only saw him at the last minute. No breaks on my trike of course, never needed them, till now! The only thing to do, avoidance, I turned the handle bars. Now tricycles don't take kindly to sharp left hand manoeuvres, or any other kind come to think of it. Although I had spent endless hours practicing on two wheels, enabled by solid rubber tyres, I couldn't handle the G force. The autumn leaves added to the skid potential of the solid tyres .The trike went left and the rider went straight over the handle bars, bounced off the path and nature supplied the brakes. A tree, my head and contact, the perfect way to test Newton's First Law of Motion, also known as the Law of Inertia, which states that an object's velocity will not change unless it is acted on by an outside force. This means that an object at rest will stay at rest until a force causes it to move. Likewise, an object in motion will stay in motion until a force acts on it and causes its velocity to change. Well I hope you get the general idea! The old guy was noticeably shocked and seemed deeply concerned about the flying Ginger missile which had flown past him. But I was a tough sort of a kid. I feigned normality, despite the extreme egg developing on my forehead.

'Are you all right son', said the old guy. I'm fine' I lied and limped off? Wait a wee minute, 'what was that pain in my leg and why are my shorts feeling wet', I thought? I put my hand into my pocket and touched my favourite object. No, you are wrong and you have a mind like a poo bucket. The item I refer to was my best metal plane, about two inches long with a V tail plane which was now embedded in my leg. Now why did I not tell anybody about the plane or my leg, especially my Mum? She would give me lots of juice, cakes and sympathy and I could watch TV for a week while I recovered. No, that was not an option. My immediate thought was what to tell her about the hole in my shorts, school shorts, not cheap and in those days and we were not well off financially. First problem, I was not allowed to be in the hospital grounds on my own in case there were dirty old men with walking sticks, her words not mine. Secondly, the whole episode was my own fault and I had intangible feelings of guilt where the old guy was concerned and thirdly, I had been told about carrying the toy in pocket. 'You'll fall off your trike and it will stick into you or something' she would say, and don't you just hate it when grownups are right. So 'Mum's the word', meaning don't tell anybody. It may have been someone in a similar predicament as me that instigated that saying!

 What happened to the trike? I went back later and found it in the bushes, hidden from view, a lucky break I suppose. I don't even think the old guy knew there was a trike involved. Never saw him again anyway. Hope he didn't have a heart attack. I could have had more guilt. See that's the way I think, fantasising about things that may or may not have happened. It is quite exhausting thinking this bike, and very much a personality trait of the addict in me.

Now, what's next, oh yes, the Bicycle. It took another year and the progression to two wheels for this particular episode to transpire.

FOUR

I had a second hand bike as were all my things, oh poor 'badly done to' wee me! But my parents were not well off despite us being middle class. No credit cards in those days, just cash. When we ran out of money in the 1950 to 60 era we did not eat or go on holiday. In fact we had no television until I was four and they only broadcast programs for a couple of hours per day. We listened to the radio a lot which kept my Mum, Sister and me up to date with the latest 'POP' songs. Dad only played his seventy eight records on the phonogram.

I remember singing along to tunes like the Laughing Policeman and the Teddy Bears Picnic. Oh the simplicity of life back then when we were hardened to Ice on the inside of the windows in the early winter mornings. Getting up, washed and dressed in record time before our wee bodies iced over. Maybe that's why people think all Scots people are Blue!

Back to the bicycle. It was a Hercules and lived up to its name regarding this incident. My transition from trike to bike was a fairly smooth ride, pun intended. My balance seemed to be of a particularly adequate standard, proved by my ability for riding a bike, playing ball games and shooting with bows and arrows and air pistols.

That did not help on this particular day as I hurtled out of the hospital boiler room gates into the road outside. I would have been fine if it had not been for the helmet. Wearing a helmet when riding your bike is so much safer according to the rules these days. Not that day though, I had it pulled over my ears to keep out the cold as I am susceptible to ear ache. It was my

Mum's idea of course, no cold air nor soundwaves either! I
don't suppose she knew I was going to fly out of the grounds
of the hospital on my bike. Some Mothers just have no
foresight when it comes to kids. Anyway the hole I created in
the side of the Turnbull and Wilson furniture van was one to
be proud of, and all due to my swanky new helmet. I don't
know how long I was out but the next thing I remember was
the very worried face of a bloke I had never seen before. He
was insisting I went to hospital, the fool, didn't he know how
much trouble I would be in for not being careful! I refused,
here I went again, same old story, better to avoid retribution,
punishment and scolding, than do the sensible thing. Guilt,
remorse and fear, once again, prevent me from facing reality.
Incident three involved a sledge and a downhill slalom. My
parents were always very caring and attentive to my needs as
a little boy. I know now that they both really did love me, but
that is so very difficult to see when one is self obsessed. I saw
only things that were centred on me. However in retrospect I
can also see how this incident highlights the conflicts of care
between my parents for their son's wellbeing. It has brought
me to an understanding of the complicated requirements of
parenthood.
I never felt I came up to my Father's expectations. I kept
trying throughout my life but never recognised the signs of
love and care given out by my father and therefore never
experienced the adulation of pleasing my Dad. Maybe he was
proud of his son's achievements. I am sure today that he was
on many occasions. But I had the grandiose desire to be on
top of the game at all times. I felt everything so acutely

especially when the signs indicated that I hadn't quite made the grade. I often felt he was disappointed in me. Not very good for my feelings of self worth.

My Mother on the other hand was very protective. I remember her taking my side when Dad thought that there was a problem, all be it big or small. So the conflict between parents became an issue as I don't handle conflict very well as a supersensitive human being. I like to please people into a state of tranquillity for the benefit of my own feelings. So who would I choose? My Mum or my Dad! My Mum of course, she was the one who was around when the going got tough as my Dad worked and she was the ever loving Mother and housekeeper. A role that thankfully is not so prevalent in these days of equality.

Another observation which came to me in later years was my reactions to being scolded for any misdemeanour. If my Dad indicated his displeasure at my actions or behaviour I would be bad tempered and stomp around the place like a wounded bear with a sore head. On the flip side, if my Mum told me off it was the end of the world, creating feelings of worthlessness, self-loathing and regret.

I suppose on reflection and analysis of the events, these are quite normal reactions to two completely different relationships. My feelings of indifference towards my Father, and my lack of understanding of his love for me as his son. Did he know how to love me? I'm not so sure he did!

It is very difficult to be a parent, I know that now after 40 years experience of the ups and downs, fears and joys of caring and sharing as they have grown up.

This particular episode with the sledge started as an innocent morning out on Blackford Hill in the middle of Edinburgh. It was close to where we lived in the area of Morningside so we had walked together as a family, My Mum, Dad, Sister Hilary and me. Oh and I almost forgot the reason for the walk, we took the dog, Copper. He was a lovely pedigree Boxer, who was as much a part of the family as any of us.

Those days in Scotland you could guarantee snow in the winter months. At least six inches deep, and stayed with us for a month or so each year.

So wellies on and taking turns to tow the sledge behind or even get the dog to pull it, which was never a success but hilariously funny as he always went his way which generally would be back the way we came, woof, woof.

The hill was about a mile away and I was about four years old at the time, so a long way for my wee legs, which were suitably attired in my black wellies with big thick socks to keep out the cold. Until the snow, which in parts was deeper than the wellington boots were tall, would find its way over the top and down to make soggy socks. Not very comfortable but when you are out for fun and excitement would never put us off.

All went well when we reached Blackford pond, which was frozen over as is the norm for that time of year. In fact we often ice skated on there without health and safety consideration, only the common sense of our parents to rely on. Oh how things have changed, I expect now there would have to be a risk assessment, committee meetings and expensive signs placed around the pond warning of the dangers. Whatever happened to personal responsibility?

We passed by the frozen pond that looked like the top of a Christmas cake with tasty icing and the prospect of marzipan delight underneath.

On up the hill which was quite a climb for a wee four year old but the promise of sledging drove me on to keep up with the big people. I was very excited and probably experiencing an adrenaline rush maybe for the first time in my life and I enjoyed the feeling. Adrenaline junky in the making!!

Quite a climb and time for sledging. My Mum was first to go down the hill. Off she went like a bat out of hell, towards the bottom. The hill was steep, maybe 3 in 1 with a path at the end followed by a barbed wire fence with sturdy posts. I saw her dig her heels in near the path as she was in a sitting position. No problem, as she stood after stopping and she turned with an immense smile on her face.

Next, my Dad went down on his own with the same result. Everyone was having a great time including my sister, Hilary, who careered to the bottom in tandem with my Dad on the back and my sister steering. This was contrary to my Mum's fears that it would end in disaster, but Dad was more confident in a positive outcome. Both of them fell off at the end amongst squeals of delight from all and sundry.

Now, wee Arthur wants a go. So it was the same again, Dad assuring Mum all shall be well. I took up position on the front with my Dad behind holding me round the waist. I have to admit I felt terrified, especially listening to my Mum's fears and predictions of impending disaster.

We were off, faster and faster, it seemed like a hundred miles an hour, not that I knew what that felt like! We approached the bottom looming ever nearer, I began to think it might be time for my Dad to put the boot brakes on. I looked up and then around to see my Dad sitting on his posterior some fifty yards back up the slope. He seemed to be waving and shouting suggestions about bailing out falling off, anything but the prospect of his wee son crashing into the barbed wire fence which was looming larger by the moment. But the opportunity to part company with the sledge was long gone as I looked to the front just in time to visualise the fence post make contact with my foot and then my head. Luckily I had a hat on tied down with a thick scarf.

There were tears and pain from the shock, bruising and sprained ankle. I actually don't remember the pain but I do remember the emotional conflict between my Mum and Dad. They were at each other's throats for quite a while as Mum said 'I told you so', followed by Dad's desperate attempts to justify the accidental nature if the incident.

All I wanted was to hear my parents being friendly. I know now that it terrified me that they were at odds with each other, and the feelings of insecurity coupled with the whole situation.

It is today a very significant episode in my life when it comes to realising how I rationalise situations and why I hid my feelings for many years to come. Another incident that structured my need to find an easy fix for my emotional traumas in life to come. I found the answer in addiction to mind altering chemistry at the age of fourteen.

SIX

Physical traumas were a problem but the emotional consequence to a supersensitive wee soul like myself were quite devastating. I never learnt how to handle personal conflict either with other people or between them. I had a very naïve perception of a perfect world and if it was balanced then I would be also.

People pleasing can be a dangerous attribute as I found out at the age of seven. My sister was also a victim to these following experiences.

A bazaar family lived across the road from our home in Cluny Place in Morningside, Edinburgh. The year when the incidents took place was 1957. I probably cannot give his second name, but Kenneth the male child in the family seemed to have a very strange and intimate relationship with his mother. They would hold hands when out and about. Now in those days that's ok if you were maybe let's say, seven or had some learning disability, but he had neither. He was sixteen years old and essentially perfectly normal. However things he did with the other children in the street, including his sister were far from acceptable as I found out later in life. Although, even at that tender age, I knew in the back of my mind that they were not essentially good things that were taking place because we were sworn to secrecy by the perpetrator, sixteen year old Kenneth. It was a secret club and was held in his bedroom under a made up tent.

We were all required to expose our private parts and he would fiddle with them and get us to do the same to him. This went on for quite some period of time and I cannot remember how or why it stopped.

To be honest the incidents did not really affect me in a negative way but the secrecy did play a part in my feelings of guilt. I knew that secrets from my parents meant that something was inherently wrong with my participation in these depraved activities. I would like to find it in my heart to forgive. He went to the same school as me and some 50 years later my sister and I found a picture of him and his family who now live in South Africa. So maybe he did face his demons in the end, who knows. 'He is more to be pitied than scorned', as Billy Connolly, the Scottish comedian, would say.

SEVEN

Cluny Place was a fantastic place to start my journey in life and I remember many incidents which could be considered to be a wee bit naughty.

I loved playing outside, and there was never a problem with abduction, paedophiles or drug addicts roaming the streets ready to pounce on the unsuspecting victim. I actually don't think things were so very different then than now, but we hear all about the seedy side of life through the ever available media in 2014.

Playing when you are a young lad is an all time consuming project so there was little time to consider taking off the muddy shoes or willies to go for a pee in the toilet.

Consequently there grew a bush at the front window in the corner of the front garden so I would check the area and piddle in the corner out of sight from nosy neighbours and scolding parents. At least I thought I was being clever until I got a proper ticking off from my Mum who obviously had seen me on several occasions while she used the vacuum cleaner and dusted in the front room.

I was threatened with disciplinary grounding if I did not use the toilet so I changed the venue for my solicitous urination and went 50 yards down the road to the hospital grounds. It really would have been so much easier to take off my wellies, but not as naughty I suppose. There was a wee bit of the rebel without a cause emerging I think!!

Hilary and I got adjustable roller skates for Christmas one year, along with a Hoola Hoop each. We had endless hours of fun for years to come with both presents. My competitive nature came to the fore with each item and I strived to be better than Hilary at both, spending endless hours practicing. I could do over a thousand revolutions of the Hoola Hoop, which was quite an achievement both physically and mentally considering I was about eight. Mathematical genius obviously ran in the family.

Cluny place also housed my first romantic obsession in the form, beautiful form, of Sandra Sinclair. The dog got walked every day at just the time she disembarked the school bus, so I could walk home with her. How pissed off was I when she

Learning Billiards aged seven

School Life 1955 to 1967
EIGHT

I went to a private school in Edinburgh called George Watson's Boys College (GWBC). It was one of a collection of schools set up by the Merchant Company of Edinburgh to provide education for the children of the business sector merchants.

There were four colleges in the group, GWBC, George Watson's Ladies, Daniel Stewarts, and Mary Erskine's. They were all good fee paying schools with a proven standard of results.

A number of students each year attained entry to Oxford and Cambridge Universities. The principal of GWBC was a man called Roger Young, who received a knighthood for his services to education. I think that is about the time knighthoods took a dive downhill, culminating in perverts and paedophiles getting honoured for their services to children in the year 2014! What a joke it all is these days. Poor Queen must be devastated to have given these monsters honours. Maybe she should have a closer look at who her advisors have been.

I had to sit a test to be allowed to attend the college. A wee bit of counting, reading, drawing, playing with bricks, that sort of thing. With my performance I was destined to become one of the elite and privileged of the world. Maybe not! Actually definitely not!

On reflection I think they looked at the ability of the parents to pay and their status in the community. My Dad was the principal Actuary with a large insurance company, the Friends

Provident, actually the only Actuary, which is pretty principal, really. So I imagine there was no hiccup there as far as the school was concerned. My Grandfather may also have been an influence.

His name was Robert Robertson, a Grand Master of the Lodge and a prominent Lawyer with a large firm of Solicitors in Edinburgh. However, he wanted me to go to Fettes College, the school for children of Solicitors in the City. But my Dad was adamant that I should go to Watson's instead. My Dad won the day. Such a load of privilege crap as I believe that all children should have access to a level playing field of education, but what do I know!

I passed, surprise, and off I went to school. It was about a mile and a half from our home in Cluny Place, Morningside, so My Mum and I would set off on foot as we did not have a car. Winter or summer, no matter what the weather. Rain, shine, snow or sleet, there was no avoiding the pleasures of getting to school. I loved school after the emotional trauma of letting go of my Mother's apron strings. Usually balling and crying like loads of kids being ripped from their secure environment to be placed in a room with 29 other individuals in the same condition. Poor teachers, ha ha! It's like getting your own back before 'it' has even happened.

School memories are a random recollection of bazaar moments in formative years. I enjoyed the first three years of school. The first class teacher was a lady called Mrs. Black. She was petite and very kind and one day we all had to pour the cream off the top of our third of a pint milk bottles into a container. The container was passed to the first child who had to shake it vigorously for about ten seconds and then pass it to your neighbour to do the same. Right round the class of thirty children. Good way to use up time in the classroom I reckon. We were making butter to put on some biscuits. You can see I became cynical over the years, very possibly being married to two teachers. I feel for all partners of the teaching profession as they must be the most boring people to talk to in the world. They are either 'know it all' people or persistently talk about pupils when you have no idea who they are, or winging about colleagues and school policies. Oh, and how hard the job is and how long the hours. There you go I feel better I have got that off my chest.

NINE

Back to random memories. As I mentioned my first three years were great due to the fact that the teachers I had were kind, caring and compassionate. That was all to change when Miss Davidson entered the fray. She used to play badminton with my Dad, and, if I got the vibes right, she fancied my Father. He would have nothing to do with her though as he was a faithful husband. Which is just as well as my Mum was never a person to mess with. She was tough when it came to the crunch.

This teacher was to be my first experience of a 'complete bitch' in my life and I suffered as a consequence.

She kept me in to finish work, dropped my grades and marks and after a year of her undivided attention I went from a happy child at school to one who dreaded going in each day. The ultimate humiliation was to be dropped a class at the age of nine and I never recovered from the experience of losing my class mates.

I made new acquaintances in the bottom class but they had different values and less of a healthy work ethic than my previous peers.

So thank you Miss Davidson and with a bit of luck you will be partying with the devil tonight and every night. You had a significant effect on ruining my life.

I actually think teachers should be brought to account for their irresponsible actions upon students.

Enough about her, my next teacher had a doctorate in something but it was not education as he stank of whisky and had a habit of getting up close when examining a student's work. When he spoke we used to say an umbrella would be an asset as he spat as he spoke. Gaud it was disgusting, pass the handkerchief please. Not to wipe away the tears but the spit, yuk, just thinking about it.

Miracle of miracles I worked hard in the next year and passed my 'Eleven Plus' as they called it then. A set of exams designed to assess your ability for entry into the senior school from preparatory. I passed with the distinction of being top in Latin which I promptly dropped in favour of Woodwork, technical drawing and metal work. All were my passions and I have always since been fairly proficient in the practical side of life. Which to me, is profoundly more interesting than a dead language.

I went on from there to successfully fail all but three of my O'level exams. As a consequence I had to re-sit them the next passes in all. Clever boy, not!

Sport during these years became an important part of my life as I felt I was useless at academic study. The proof was there after all, endorsed by the dreadful teachers allotted to the lower classes by this wonderful 'head up it's arse' school, run by an egotistical Knight who seemed only consumed by self interest. Personal opinion of course.

Tennis is my favourite sport as a result of my parents taking me to Westhall Tennis Club every weekend in the summer months from the age of nothing, along with my sister Hilary and an army of other children.

It was behind the pavilion at Westhall that I had my first kiss. Instigated by my darling sister who forced my attentions onto another six year old, thankfully female. It was not for my benefit or the poor victim of my attentions, but for my sister's amusement accompanied by her squeals of delight at having manipulated her wee brother into an embarrassing situation. As for other sports, I also reached a reasonable standard playing squash, cricket and golf.

TEN

Fights at school were absolutely forbidden but were conducted in secret on many occasions. I had my share but I am ashamed to say the only one I lost was in full view of Mr. Taylor, the Maths teacher.

A lad from the year above me had stolen our football and it seemed up to me to be the hero, impetuous fool that I was, but I have always hated bullying and that is what this was as they were all bigger than us. I took him on and had him squawking for mercy on the ground with his arm up his back and my foot on his neck. Big mistake, I let him go. Next thing I knew I had his arm around my neck and he endeavoured to snap my vertebra. I tried not to, but the tears of pain rolled down my cheek and I was beaten. However I was revered by my mates as a bit of a hero for having a go, but it didn't feel that way to me, not with my twisted neck muscles and embarrassment of tears.

Then of course there was the teacher, Mr Taylor. He had a reputation for giving boys the cane across the backside. We used to compare bruises on our bums at swimming in the changing rooms. This today or course would be tantamount to child abuse and would have landed him in court. But to give him his due he commanded great respect despite the canings and he was a really good maths teacher.

He called me in after the lunch break when the incident had happened and I have to say I was pooping bricks, thinking I would get another beating along with the humiliation of losing the fight.

'Biggs' he roared and I came skulking along with my tail between my legs to face the music.

He said to me 'If I ever see you fighting again and letting a larger opponent get up off the ground when you have him beaten I will undoubtedly give you a caning, now go and sit down you have maths to learn'. I could not believe what he was saying or believe my luck. That is definitely one of the most valuable lessons I have learned. If you have to fight then make sure the other guy stays down when you get him down. Compassion and conflict really do not make comfortable bedfellows.

On reflection there are so many differences to schooling and teaching today. In my days of education the belt, cane, slipper or gym shoe were common place punishments. They did command a certain fearful respect from the students. However bullying by the teacher in the classroom did occur and I was party to such abuse along with every other student who was taught by Mr. Moyes, the french and history teacher. He would set us tests and anybody who achieved less than 50% would be hauled to the front of the class and receive two lashes of the belt, the taws they called it in Scotland. A leather strap/belt which had a split end. Sometimes our wrists would bleed and if you pulled away he kept going until he got a good swipe. Now that is bullying. I had several weeks off school because I lived in fear of this man and his tactics. He was fired in the end after many letters of complaint from the parents of the victims.

I was taken every other day to the doctors with a pain in my tummy. Each time I was interrogated by my mother and father to find out the cause but it was three weeks before I revealed the true problem. It was at that point that my parents wrote a letter of complaint to the school and an investigation ensued culminating in the pressured resignation of Mr. Moyes and his instrument of torture.

The school itself had a very grandiose atmosphere with a splendid building and massive grounds. They even had air raid shelters at the bottom of the playing fields for the evacuation of the staff and pupils in the event of war time German assaults on Edinburgh during world war two.

I loved the summer months when we were allowed to play on the fields at lunch time as the winter alternative were the quadrangles which really did not have enough room to allow for football games at break times.

In the winter if it snowed everybody turned up an hour before school started and stayed for an hour after to have snow ball fights between the years. First, third and sixth year against the second, fourth and fifth year pupils. It was a massive fight with two to three hundred boys and the equivalent number of snow and ice balls flying from side to side at any given time. You were going to get hit, just as long as you could identify and dodge the ice balls, they were dangerous and there would be forty or fifty casualties per fight of varying degrees. Each side also trying to take hostages who were duly rolled and had ice balls put inside their clothing which was very painful and you might have to sit in wet clothes all day if it was the morning battle.

I have always been very competitive and that in itself became a problem both at school and at home. I always wanted to achieve but never felt I came up to other people's expectations. So disappointment featured as a great part of my early years. It takes a great deal of self belief and self worth to over-ride the opinions of other people. Drink took all the fears and inadequacies away.

It became a safe haven for me until the haven became a prison of the mind, soul and spirit.

School days were a mixture of academic struggle, sporting achievements playing for the first tennis, squash and cricket teams, second team in the rugby and a lot of good friends and fellowship.

Therefore not all bad, although I never felt I came up to scratch with regards to the expectations of my parents but my Dad in particular.

My early schooling consisted of learning the times tables. Going around the class room reciting them until the response to a multiplication problem became automatic. English was spelling as it is and not in phonic or text form as I witness today in young people's writing.

Discipline was harsh as I mentioned before but we knew here the boundaries lay, clear cut acceptability of our moral standards and behaviour. We were brought up to be polite and respectful to our elders and swearing of any sort was socially unacceptable. Nowadays it seems the barriers have been lifted by media, stretching the boundaries of acceptability.

The question I ask myself now, is this social progress or regress.

Back in the 1960's calculations were by hard strive and mental ability, no calculators, only slide rules and logarithms. It is interesting to note that the latest innovation in the Arabic world is a process called Maths Genius which is churning out some prestigious results amongst the pupils introduced to the new idea. The amazing fact about this innovative idea is that they are learning and using the abacus, which must have been around for at least two thousand years. Now that is progress.

GWBC was and still is a good school if you are one of the winners academically but the poorest teachers were always allocated the poorest students unlike state schools which have a much different ethic. However there are pros and cons to both systems. State schools can be guilty of holding back the more gifted as a consequence of making more effort with the more troublesome students.

Academically I have always been a very slow reader and those who criticised or humiliated me for my inabilities may you all forever regret your opinions. I could not seem to find a smooth process which read the words and eventually spit them out of my mouth. Reading out loud has always been one of primary fears. I felt intense feelings of guilt about these inadequacies, which is not a building block for one's self worth.

I remember when I was in class at school and I knew the answer to a question I behaved like 'Donkey' in the film

Shrek, almost jumping up and down thinking 'pick me, pick me'.

There is also the flip side on the scenario where if I did not know the answer I wanted to be swallowed up and disappear for fear of being selected.

During my education at Watson's College we had the opportunity to go on cruises with other schools on ships called the Dunera and the Dunedin. One went to Moscow, Lenningrad (now St. Petersburgh) Stolkholme and Copenhagen. The other cruise went to Santander in Spain, Cadiz and Oporto in Portugal.

There were eight hundred pupils from various school from around the world including, Canada, France, England, Wales and Scotland. It must have been a nightmare for our teachers as we constantly battled with other nations and schools for supremacy of the ship and recreation areas. The adversity came in the form of pillow fights and general pushing and shoving but never deteriorated into all out violence. In fact most of it was a pretty innocuous disorder.

Moscow definitely held the position of most interesting place for a young lad like me. I remember being anxious about the kind of food we would get but it turned out to be very similar to British fayre.

The buildings were bigger and fancier than any I had seen in my life and we visited the Kremlin beside the Red Square, all of which I had only heard of as it was 1964 and the news on TV was not my favourite program. We queued to see Lenin's body in the Kremlin which I have to say did not move me in any way as I was clueless about his importance in European history.

There were KGB, Russian Secret police men, on every street corner and we had been warned not to step out of line as we could be arrested for the simplest of misdemeanours. One of which, we were informed was to sell any of our clothes or shoes to the local people. We were approached by quite a few young people to swap our shoes and jumpers for the exchange of some Roubles (currency) but with the previous warnings from our teachers we were too frightened.

I feel very privileged to have experienced these trips at that time because to go abroad in the early sixties was a rarity. It cost my sixty pounds for the two week trip which I had to save from my pocket money and a withdrawal from my savings account.

Random Recollections of My Teenage Years
ELEVEN

At the age of twelve we moved house from Cluny Place, Morningside to Pentland Terrace which is on the main road south from Edinburgh on the outskirts in an area between Buckston and Greenbank.

The move had been a wee bit traumatic for me as I would be leaving my friends in the street, and also the girl of my fantasy, Sandra. But I was older now and had many friends from school and especially from the church in Greenbank parish. I had been introduced to the fellowship there by my Mother who was a Christian, unlike my Father who proclaimed himself as a Humanist.

In the 1960's the communities in Edinburgh revolved around your parish church, unless of course you lived in one of the answers to the population boom, the high rise flats. Our nearest one they called Oxgangs. The very nature of the name can conjure up connotations of gangland and it had just that, a gang of thugs who challenged our existence at every opportunity.

Our church had a youth club and it was the centre of our weekend discos and dances. My sister, who is three years older than me, was in the Greenbank gang which was made up of her friends from all different schools but lived in the area and all went to the same church and youth club.

 The next group or gang as it turned out to be, contained all my pals. I think we had about fifty in each group, boys and girls. We were not thugs or anything like it but you had to defend your area and youth club against the aggressive intrusion of the Oxgangers, who called themselves the 'Bar Ox'.

Fights at the dances were quite a regular occurrence and sometimes it was a bit like the wild west as chairs and fists flew in all directions. We never lost and sometimes teamed up with the Fairmilehead church gang to form a formidable force to be reckoned with.

I was never fighter unless I had to defend myself and tended to hang around with my best mate Graham who was an ABA lightweight boxing champion. A handy guy to have around in a rumble, and the boyfriend of my childhood sweetheart, Sandra Sinclair. She was gorgeous and lived only a few doors from us in Cluny Place. Never kissed her unfortunately but she was my first crush which lasts until today even though I have not seen her for Fifty years.

I had a lot of girlfriends who never lasted long, never more than six months. I was very shy of asking girls out in fear of rejection which I just could not handle. It was not until I met Elaine that I had a long term relationship. A pretty wee lass whom I eventually married seven years after we met.

The move to Pentland Terrace had its advantages. I had a brilliant room with the attic space access and a box room which my father used as a dark room for his photography. I loved helping him to develop his black and white images into prints. We used to lay them out on newspaper over night to dry and my job after that was to touch up the dust spots with varying shades of grey. Not like today when it is all done on a computer program which does all sorts of wonderful things

but I feel takes away the essential element of human error in
photography.

I loved the anxious moments awaiting the return of the
colour film from the Kodak factory. The camera only took 35
mm film, not like the cameras today which take digital images
that can be discarded at the flick of a switch. We took the
snap and there would be no turning back. The ultimate
resulted in waiting to see the outcome several weeks later
when the arrived back in the post as a slide or a print.

I had had a big cut down four poster bed since I was four
years old. The posts were removed but it left a large space
under the bed of some eighteen inches. My sister told me
when I was five that if I did not do as she wanted the monster
under the bed would put out a hairy arm and drag me
underneath. In consequence I always took a running jump to
land on the bed and avoid the hairy hand of the beast
underneath. I still at sixty four years old worry about beds
with large storage spaces below.

TWELVE

My mother always did the wall papering in the house. She showed me how to do it and the first room I endeavoured to tackle was my sister's room. I was twelve at the time. I was told to put on old clothes but in my impatience I just went ahead in my good school uniform. It was a drop match of eighteen inches, so quite tricky for a novice. I duly went about the task with great enthusiasm, so much so that I was overheating and thought it a good idea to open the window. I pasted the paper, waited the ten minutes for it to soak in and then lifted the piece to carry towards the wall. Nobody had suggested that one should carry the paper with the pasted side facing the wall. The wind blew in the window and pasted the roll to my Sunday best clothes, face and hands. Lesson one was complete.

Smoking in the sixties was a cool thing to do. All the film stars such as, Cowboys, James Bond AKA 007, Comedians, women and men had a fag hanging from their mouths as they spoke, waved them around and generally spoke real tough while puffing on a ciggie. Sounded like a good idea to me so when I was ten I pinched my Dad's Players Medium Navy Cut, the kind they used to give away free to the sailors. Very strong and had no tip. I remember feeling dizzy, sick and generally crap but I persevered because I wanted to fit in. Big mistake as I had no idea I was an addict. Did I ever get caught I hear you asking. Yes I did at a very early stage as I was blowing the smoke out of my first floor bedroom window, I was ten years

old at the time. Unfortunately for me I did not realise my
Mum was in the garden talking to a neighbour.

'Is your bedroom on fire' shouted my mother.

I could have shot under the four poster bed, died, anything
but get caught. What could I have said in reply?

I got such a ticking off, a reduction in pocket money and
grounded to do more homework. It still did not stop me
though. I seemed to have a self destruct button even then. It
was another thirty years before I finally learned my lesson
and gave up the weed.

Number 56 Pentland Terrace had an air raid bunker under the
garage. That was my next wee cubby hole to develop my
devious behaviour. I even painted it out and put a seat in to
provide comfort while I performed my sneaky behaviour and
puffed like a proverbial steam train. By this time I had taken a
leaf out of 007's book and started to smoke posh fags in order
to emulate James Bond. He always got the girls after all is said
and done. St Mauritz   tipped cigarettes, the only thing
missing was the shaken not stirred Vodka Martini, but it was
not long before that became a part of the underground
shelter rituals.

I had my first experience with alcohol at the age of fourteen.
Two cans of McEwen's export. Vile taste but became my new
wow factor which I made my best friend for years to come,
but more about the alcoholism later.

Recreational activities at this age centred around the golf
course across the road, Mortonhall where my Dad was
captain so I was well known by all the members as the
captain's son.

I also played tennis in the same area at a club just down the road where there were a mixed group of friends. The golf club had no female members of my own age so we tended to socialise at the tennis club with a few wild moments. Mostly centred around the changing rooms and showers, so I will leave that up to your imagination to make of it what you will. The church backed onto the tennis club so most of the socialising was in the same area needing little or no transport although we all had bikes and went for runs at the weekends and holidays.

Our house over looked the Pentland hills, hence the street name. We spent a lot of time walking and going for picnics, sometimes with our parents but mostly with our friends now that we were older.

My pals and I got caught out one time while having a pleasant day on the hillside. A group of thugs from the afore mentioned Oxgangs were out for the day as well, but not for the same reasons as we were, they were out for bother.

Don, Ian and I had taken three girls out for a walk on the Sunday afternoon. There was an ice cream van nearby so Ian stayed with the girls as we had seen the other gang in the distance and thought it safer for one of us to stay with our girls friends while Don and I went for the ice creams.

We walked down to the van where the queue was quite lengthy. We were all in party mood and the sun shone on all the families out for a pleasant afternoon stroll. Kiddie's playing football or rounders with their mums and dads. Sounds of happiness and laughter until it all went eerily quiet. We never thought any more about it until there were shouts and screams from not far away. There seemed to be chaos over by the spot where we had left the others. People running about in turmoil and then we heard our names being called out by the girls. Never mind the ice creams we set off in the direction of our pals but by the time we got there the Oxgangs yobbos had fled and all that we could see was our pal Ian with blood all over his head and face lying unconscious on the ground. An ambulance and the police were called but the culprits had long gone but we had an idea who they were and it was a year later before we exacted retribution. The chance for revenge wasn't planned it just landed in our lap like a gift from the Gods. Bonfire night in the Hermitage grounds near our church. We had about fifty of our friends from the Greenbank gang along with many more from Fairmilehead. I don't think the Oxgangs crew knew there were so many of us but in the end it did not matter as only half a dozen of us were needed to sort out the situation. We were having a really good time cooking baked potatoes, toasting mushroom and preparing to set off a few small fireworks when they arrived. The boys from Oxgangs were not the sharpest tools in the box. They came tooled up with knives and stones so must have had pre knowledge of our party.

The abuse started first from a distance, there must have been about twenty five of them of varying sizes and ages from fourteen to twenty. The abuse we ignored and the challenges to fight were treated as a potential threat but this time we had had enough and we were ready to retaliate if the problem persisted. Around the fire we started group in threes and fours so nothing was too obvious and they were probably too thick and over confident to suss out what was going on. We separated the girls gradually putting them into the back ground. Everything needed to seem as if we were frightened of them and that we did not want trouble. We held off as long as we could until the stones started to fly amongst our girls, which was the catalyst we needed for an excuse to let loose. We hit them in groups of four, right into the middle of their gang separating them into four sections so that they were divided and lost some of their bravado. Apple, a boxer, and a wiry guy hit them first with some orthodox boxing techniques which took them by surprise. We said nothing, nor did we shout or swear. Graham my pal and I went in next, fists flying and finally, three of the older guys in our group tore apart their biggest members. It was all over in thirty seconds, they fled still shouting abuse at us but completely disorganised and in a state of chaos and confusion. They never troubled us again, at least not for a year or so anyhow. I don't like violence, in fact I hate and fear it. There is nothing courageous about me but when I lose my temper I am capable of nearly anything drunk or sober. Must be the Scottish nature coupled with my red hair gene.

I mentioned in my early years several traumatic incidents that I am sure had a significant impact on my reactions toward my future life.

One of the most serious came in the form of a road traffic collision and I feel that it highlights my personality traits and reactions to my own shortcomings.

I made a good friend in the British Linen Bank, George Street, Edinburgh, which was one of the branches I worked in during 1968. She was called Alexandra and was the daughter of the owner of a garage just outside Edinburgh. Alex as she liked to be called, taught me a lot about banking and we became good friends over the year that I held the post of apprentice clerk.

I was eighteen and had become a legal drinker so I frequented several different hotels and bars. Alex had come up to my house in south Edinburgh and we went for a social drink in the Buckston Hotel, just a couple of drinks and she drank orange juice as she mature and sensible unlike myself. She took us in her Hillman Imp sports and on our return a Skoda van driver took the notion to do a U-turn in our path. We hit broadside at 50 MPH. now an Imp was the size of a wee Mini and the van needless to say was the size of a sturdy van. We came off worse and I was catapulted through the windscreen but somehow I did not go all the way through. On my return journey back into the car the windscreen glass took the side of my face off along with half my nose.

The ambulance came and took me to the RVI hospital in Edinburgh, where, not being my luckiest day, I had to wait on a gurney trolley thing while the doctors dealt with a drug addict who had taken copious amounts of some substance and was dying before their very eyes. This was my first encounter with drug problems and the year was 1968. There was so much more to come but one could predict that the addict wo9uld have been me.

My turn came to be treated and have my face stitched back on with over one hundred stitches to re-attach my cheeks and nose. I counted them as they took them out three weeks later.

I felt no pain at all through the whole incident as my brain had switched off the receptors, through shock I suppose. The only thing I felt were the injections going into my nose to numb the area about to be stitched.

I remember being told I could get off the operating table but to avoid any mirrors until I got home as I might be upset by the state of my face. So naturally I paid no attention to anything they sai8d and the first thing I did was to look at my reflection in the glass cupboard doors in the theatre. After falling back onto the table and feeling inordinately sick I adhered to the suggestions on the doctors and nurses as they steadied my anxieties for the next few moments.

Mum and Dad had been called by the Alex who had accompanied me to the hospital. Poor lassie was in a terrible state mentally but only had a wee cut on her nose. She had been wearing a seat belt and I had not as they were not yet a legal requirement at the time. I guess I am a great example of self will run riot and outright masculine stupidity, 'it will never happen to me, ha ha'.

When I look back on this incident I am quite shocked to find that from the moment after the initial shock of seeing my face in the cupboard door I began to love the attention and sympathies of all my friends and family.

My Sister, Hillary, passed out when she came in to look at the damage to my face and it must have been very traumatic for my parents to be summoned to the hospital because their son had been involved in a road traffic collision. To see me lying in the A&E covered in bandages saturated with blood. I never looked the same again, but as I said, I loved the attention, and paraded my scars like trophies won in the heat of battle. The shattered glass from the windscreen had embedded itself in my gums, cheeks, brow and nose but miraculously had missed my eyes by a millimetre. I spat out pieces of the glass for four weeks after the accident as the swelling gradually released the sparkly foreign invaders. I also picked out pieces of shard glass from my nose as it healed over them. These wee devils erupted in the form of spots for at least ten years as they came to the surface. It became quite good fun digging them out and saving them for posterity, more trophies, I guess.

The car crash happened in the summer of 1968, a few months after my eighteenth birthday in the April. The birthday party took place in my house in Pentland Terrace, Edinburgh. It boasted a theme of 'Black and White' and all of the guests came in costume, wearing black and white hats or dressed as Zebra crossings etc. I remember feeling very grown up as we all met for the first time in the local hotel bar. My first legal drink ever, in public. My friends had all been in bars since they were about sixteen but I never looked old enough, nor had the courage to chance being challenged over my age. In fact when I was twenty one I was asked about my age and I told the barman in a very indignant fashion that I had been drinking in bars for three years so he told me to come back to his in another three years. I hated and carried resentments against that bar, the barman and any bar with the name of Kings Head for decades after the incident.

2oth July 1973 Just married to Elaine

THIRTEEN
Music, the Bands and Opportunities Lost.

I grew up with music in all aspects of my life. I love listening to music. I have a very eclectic taste enjoying classical through jazz and country to pop and rap. I have a selective ear for each genre and some music calms my soul and some interpretations disturb me. It also depends greatly on how I feel at any moment in time.

My parents both played the piano. My Mother was a WREN and played for the troops during the world war two. She received a silk purse presented to her by Princess Elizabeth who was crowned Queen in 1953. Her sixty five year old son is still waiting for her to abdicate and it is June 2014. She could play anything from Honky-tonk to the Classics.

My Father taught himself and became fairly accomplished at some classical pieces. He also played the clarinet, inspired by Acker Bilk back in the 1950's

I remember my Mother buying an accordion which she called her 'Squeeze Box'. I think the nick name came from the band called the Who, which was a massive pop hit around 1966.

At family parties and all social gatherings in our house friends and neighbours alike would ply my Mother with gin and tonics in order to persuade her to get out the 'Squeeze Box' and play some Scottish jigs and reels. I was inspired by all this to take up a musical instrument after being forced into piano lesson at the age of nine. I unfortunately learned to hate the piano as my teacher, a neighbour across the road called Miss Simington, stabbed my fingers every time I hit a wrong note. My goodness she was a skinny, scary woman.

I am surprised I continued my interest in music after that introduction. I think I have an internal implant in my head that responds to rhythm and melody. My next adventure in music was inspired by two television programs, the adventures of William Tell who was a sort of Robin Hood of the Swiss Alps, in today's terms he would be labelled a terrorist I expect as he fought for the rights of the oppressed. The theme tune for the program was the William Tell overture by Rossini, This was also the theme for the Lone Ranger with his sidekick Tonto. Tonto is Spanish for Stupid I learned some fifty years later. So while the Lone Ranger rode around shouting Tonto to his North American Indian partner, fairly racist really by today's standards.

Anyhow those two programs of the TV coupled with the theme tunes to Coronation Street and Z Cars, inspired me to take up the trumpet. I had lessons from an Eastern European guy and eventually was asked to join the orchestra at school. I declined this offer even though my grandiose personality trait told me how important I would become, but fear held me back. I had a great desire to be the centre of attention in life but the fear of failure and criticism once again prevented me from doing what I really wanted to do.

When I moved to Pentland Terrace I became the neighbour of a school friend Tommy. His Dad owned a garage and had loads of money. He spoiled Tommy financially and deprived him of any emotional guidance. His Father became the Lord Mayor of Edinburgh and I remember the registration of his Rolls Royce, GHM 97. One of the first personalised plates in Edinburgh, which I think speaks volumes about his ego.

Tommy played the Guitar, the electric guitar, and in the early sixties this instrument was brand new to the music scene, with a solid body and many unique designs. Top of the Pops had become an institution on the TV highlighting all the latest trends in Pop music and fashion. I was desperate to learn the guitar and consequently bought my own instrument, a Fender Copy. Tommy taught me to play and the trumpet took a backseat for the next fifty years of my life.

I became friends with another guy at school called Arthur who played the drums. We formed a band called the' Pryzym', cannot for the life of me explain why or how the name came about but it must have seemed good at the time. Don and Barry joined us. Don played the base guitar and Barry played the keyboard. I remember the first song we learned was 'Winchester Cathedral' by the New Vodival Band' which had climbed the charts in record time, excuse the pun! All recordings had progressed from 78 revolutions per minute, to 45 for single recordings and 33.3 for Long Playing records which had seven songs on each side. All made out of vinyl plastic.

We rehearsed some more tunes and eventually played a couple of pubs and entered some talent competitions, none of which we won but it was all valuable experience.

My Mother once listened to one of our practices and gave some feed back to our performance. She said my singing was a bit flat band the drummer ran away with his timing. I obsessed about those comments for years to come and it had a very negative effect on me. However after discovering Alcohol I could put those fears aside and believed my performance improved after a few whiskies. I was only sixteen at the time and started to carry a quarter bottle in my guitar case, drinking it in secret before I went on stage. This was a sign of things to come but the progression of my drinking was innocuous, nobody sees Alcoholism coming, especially not the drinker.

The band moved on, people left and new guys joined, the only two constants were Don and me.

The type of music developed too from pure Pop from the charts to Folk Rock inspired by a Glasgow band called the JSD Band. The name was formed from the initials of the members, Jim, Shug and Des.

This sounded a good idea to us so we called ourselves 'Fred McCludgies Big IDEA', Ian the fiddle and base player who went on to become a lawyer and one of the most respected fiddle players and writer of music in Scotland, Don on base, mandolin and banjo, Eddie on percussion and vocals and Arthur (me) on rhythm guitar and banjo. We played a rocked up version of folk music and electrified jigs and reels. We became one of the top bands in Edinburgh in the late sixties for this type of music and played the same venues with other performers, such as Billy Connolly in the Humble Bums, Isla Sinclair and Gerry Rafferty.

There was a lot of drink fuelled stupidity went on but we had a great time and were totally irresponsible. Drink driving, drugs (cannabis mainly), fighting (usually defending our own corner in dance halls where the local gangs took offence at incomers and girls, there were the groupies and the girlfriends, neither of which had a liking for each other and showed it in a variety of different ways. Mostly name calling but sometimes physical hair pulling and the occasional cigarette stubbed out on each other. My girlfriend had one stubbed out on her face in a night club but we could not find the offender, but I still remember my fury, a desperate need for retribution and revenge. My feelings have always been very intense when it comes to injustice coupled with powerlessness over a situation. Alcohol would soon be a constant solution to my inability to handle these situations. Back in nineteen sixty nine we were approached by an agent who wanted us to go professional. I had been all for it and so was Eddie but the other two lads being nineteen respectively decided not to accept as they were at university studying, one to be a lawyer and the other an interior designer. An opportunity lost for me and Eddie but that is life.

I went on to work for Polydor records after this and became a sales and promotions rep for the East Anglia area based bin Peterborough near London. The entertainment environment played a significant part in the development of my Alcoholism. The booze was essentially free at venues where the bands and artists were performing and many of them had addiction problems themselves, so it was ideal for me to feed my addiction.

By now I did not play my guitar except to entertain myself, the days of the band were gone and we had all moved on. Later in life I rekindled me enthusiasm for playing music when I found recovery, but that would not happen for another eighteen years.

To date I have mastered the trumpet, tenor sax, soprano sax, guitar, mandolin, a wee bit piano and banjo. I don't play any of them really well but I do read music which helps me understand the theory and practical aspects of any instrument. I still would love to play the drums, so one never knows that before I kick the bucket I still have it on my list.

Heading up in my first rock band 1966 aged sixteen.

Career Choices and Technological Journey
FOURTEEN

Whilst at school we were not really advised on any career but steered in a certain direction by our choices of subjects. I think before the age of eleven I had no idea what I wanted to be when I grew up. My Father worked for an insurance company all his life and I remember him complaining about it and how he had wanted to do something else, but the salary was good and he had the responsibility of being the only provider to bring food to our table and pay the bills. I think on reflection he felt trapped in a career that he eventually hated due to the fact that there seemed no alternative.

He was a very clever man with his hands and technical brain. He built radios from spare parts and taught me to do the same. At ten years of age I built my first transistor radio from a kit which worked and I could get BBC radio programmes on it. There was no choice of alternate stations in those days as they did not exist. We had no television programmes to speak of, except the test card for at least six hours a day. The test card helped the engineers or anybody in fact to point the aerial in the correct direction for the best signal.

Satellites had not been invented as far as I know because I remember the Russians were first to put one up in space, it was called Sputnik. At the time we all thought it was a miracle where as today there are more than ten thousand satellites orbiting the earth at any one time. It is really mind boggling to us mere humans, the advancement of technology today.

I enjoyed woodwork, metal work and technical drawing. I liked art but I did not seem to have the ability to put on paper the images I carried in my head.

My Mother had chosen to be a housewife, to stay at home to look after the needs of my father, my sister and me. She used to meet up with all her friends and neighbours once or twice a week for coffee mornings. There was always a great spirit of community in Cluny Place. The street was a cul-de-sac which led to the grounds of the Astley Aynsley hospital and some lock ups where we eventually garaged our car.

My Dad took the plunge after he qualified as an Actuary with a significant salary increase and bought a brand new car one day. Everything up until then had been second hand and I mean everything. The car was an Austin Cambridge and would be very much more comfortable for our family needs. He proudly parked the car outside our house each day after work before taking it to the garage at the back.

The next thing we heard was a horrendous crashing sound. We all rushed out to find the source of the drama. A hospital ambulance driver had lost concentration and his vehicle had collided with the side of Dad's pride and joy. There was now only one side of the car left and my dad had a foul temper sometimes. This was one of those 'go and hide' moments. I had heard him swear before but this was entirely new to my ears. He was angry for days after the incident with my mum trying to calm him but to no avail.

This does not have anything to with my career but it does show the under lying anger and frustration my father seemed to be feeling. I am not sure if he was ever content. I think I have inherited this defective gene as I look back on my journey. Maybe the grass was always greener on the other side but it never was when I finally got over the fence.

The first set of O'levels I failed to work for but the fright of being left behind by my class mates seemed to spurn me into action and I passed the next year. Unfortunately the school were not so impressed with me and asked that I leave and not sit my higher in GWBC. Toffy nosed gits and my dad went mad complaining to the head master, Roger Young (later to become Sir). But to no avail as I decided for myself that I hated school anyway and left at seventeen with my 8 O'levels behind me.

My parents knew the British Linen bank manager and he also was an old Watsonian which is a former pupil of GWBC. So the old school tie got me a job in the bank. I did not really want the job but I did not meet the requirements to be flavour of the month due to the early exit from school.

I can understand my parent's disappointment as they had invested a lot of time and money to get me the best education, but I am just not an academic.

I have always read very slowly and find it difficult to find the right words when under stress. My numeric skills were good due to the fact I had a maths genius as a father. He had a very good way of helping me understand the basics for which I am very grateful.

Maybe I have always been somewhere on the lower levels of the autistic scale but they did not exist in my school days. Banking therefore would be my chosen career. I started as a clerk and progressed to a position as a teller. Serving the public directly, all the customers seemed to like me and the manager was happy with my progress. My stumbling block once again was the bank exams. Scottish law, accountancy and incredibly boring, so I found it impossible to keep focused and consequently failed all but the English higher paper. I was hauled in front of the manager who revealed his disappointment in me and how I had let my parents down. I did the only thing I could think of in my defence and told him this really is not for me and resigned. Oh dear, the son has flunked again.

Thankfully money was not a problem as I was playing every night in the band and sometimes making ten pounds per night. The bank salary was six hundred pounds per year so that was not going to be too difficult to make up if I got another job which I did in double quick time.

I went to work as the sample room manager in Munrospun Knitwear Company much to the delight of my girl friend Elaine who benefitted from Cashmere jumpers etc. at zero prices.

I stayed with them for a year, learning to crochet and knit, taught by the sample room team who were the elite in machinists and who worked in close conjunction with the designer, who was the first gay guy I had had the pleasure to encounter in the workplace or any place as far as I knew. Mr. Sommerville with the limp handshake and the penguin walk and he was really sexually rude in front of the women which I had never come across before as I was brought up not to speak of things. Very sheltered wee man I must have been. I was really quite shocked to find the girls all loved the flirtation.

The three hundred or so girls on the work floor spotted this and my eyes were opened on a daily basis when I became the primary target for their amusement. They were also as rude as possible and endeavoured to embarrass this new public school boy whenever the bosses' heads were turned the other way. I quite enjoyed it actually as it was all new to me. It was the first time I had heard the alternative word for a lady's private part, began with a C and ended with a T. I still don't like the word today and causes me to flinch when it is used by others.

FIFTEEN

Unfortunately Munrospun began to struggle against the cheaper imported goods from Asia. I was twenty one at the time, and before applying to Munrospun I had an interview for Polydor Recording Company as a sales representative. I had not been given the appointment but they said they would keep my name on file for further positions in the future. I had heard this before at interviews and just felt it was a brush off in the nicest possible way. 'Get stuffed your no good' would be how I felt on more than one occasion. I suppose they are just trying to be kind but second best is never a pleasant position to be in given any competition.

I could not have been more wrong on this instance as it was to be my saving grace from a failing company which I believe would have initiated the last in, first out rule very shortly.

When the phone call came from my new boss to be, George, the manager of the Scottish team for Polydor, I was over the moon with excitement, a dream come true to work in the industry of my greatest passion, music.

To top the cake with a cherry the first contact I would to have was an invitation to the after party of the Eurovision Song Contest which that year was being held in Edinburgh's Usher Hall.

I put on my best suit, shirt and tie to meet George at the largest, posh hotel in the west end of Princess Street. I have to say I felt very insecure approaching the hotel and asking at the door for Mr. Wishart of Polydor. I felt really overwhelmed by the atmosphere and very out of place with all the pop and media stars chatting and I think the most fervent memory was the fact they were human beings after all. The scent of stale perfume and after shave mixed with the smells of sweaty bodies made it all real and not quite as glamorous as I had first perceived when I walked in the door.

After my initiation I joined a team of five sales reps, a display agent and promotions personnel to cover Scotland and North east England plus the Cumbria district. The area was very large which entailed driving our Cortina cars at break neck speeds to get to venues, concerts and shops, which reflected our extremely immature and avant-garde attitudes. We were untouchable and also having bucket loads of fun whilst full of drugs and alcohol but it was all part and parcel of the industry in the 1970's.

This period of time was very significant in the progression of my Alcoholism. The booze would very often be on expenses or free and the company I kept all used in a similar fashion. Many of them have ended up in the same fellowship as me or members of Narcotics Anonymous (NA).

As they say in the fellowship 'if you go to a Barber's shop often enough you will end up getting a hair cut', so if you hang about with 'users' the chances are you will use too.

My Alcoholic career is jaded by dozens of embarrassing incidents some of which I remember vividly.

The company hosted a conference each year to honour the staff that had excelled in their efforts to keep Polydor as one of the leading organisations in the music business.

This particular event took place in one of the best known restaurants in London which hosted medieval meals.

We, the reps, started the evening in our hotel room at Heathrow airport, emptying the mini bar and smoking joints to kick start the adventure so by the time we got to the restaurant yours truly was fairly inebriated. But there was the promise of food to soak up the booze, however food does not soak up a combination of booze and cannabis. I was rocking and rolling, literally. The company had invited a singer along to entertain us during the meal but as I was an accomplished musician, or so I thought when I was drunk, I thought it best to join in the festivities.

I demanded the guy's guitar when he had finished his spot and duly gave a few renditions of the old songs we had played when I was in the band with my mates. The result was an embarrassed silence to which I thought 'How rude when I have so selflessly entertained them'. My boss came across and offered to introduce me to one of our latest signings from America. He called the guy over, the very man whom I had borrowed the guitar from, Steve Goodman, one of the top selling Country and Western artists in the world. I have never wanted the earth to open and swallow me whole quite so much in my life.

I started in the northern area so part of my coverage included Aberdeen at the beginning of the oil boom in 1972. Those days were an education for me with regards to partying, taking drugs and generally a life of glorious debauchery.

I caught a dose of the 'crabs' from a very willing and beautiful young lady. This was particularly bad timing and very embarrassing as I was to be married to Elaine a few months later. I had to shave off all the hair around my private parts and treat myself with vinegar. The most difficult part was to think up a good excuse to tell my wife to be on our honeymoon why my testicles and penis that resembled a plucked chicken. In those days the liberal freedom did not extend to revealing sexual oddities. Today nobody would bat an eyelid if there were rings, fairies and Christmas lights attached to external or internal parts of the body.

Elaine and I got married on the 20th July 1973 on a very wet Friday in Edinburgh in Fairmilehead parish church.

We got a cottage in Carham near Kelso and lived there for a year. My promotion in Polydor meant we had to relocate to Peterborough near London much to my wife's disgust as she had to change from a teacher in the Scottish system to the English one.

All seemed great for me and I had a very selfish attitude and no consideration for Elaine's feelings. Drinking and the high life kept my ego boosted with little compassion or thought for anyone but me.

After four years and countless humiliations I had to leave Polydor to find another job, but that was short lived and we made a decision. I worked as a rep for Monks and Crane Tools, but my drinking had become an all day event by this time and employment was unsustainable as I had become unreliable and quite dishonest. I ended with Polydor because I had started to make up orders in the house and send them into the shops without their permission, needless to say they started to complain and I ended up trying to cover up lie after lie. The same was happening with the tool company and it became necessary to plan a geographical move back to Edinburgh.

Whilst in Market Deeping Elaine became pregnant which felt like the Immaculate Conception as we had had a problem sexually since we got married. I am a very touchy feely person and Elaine was the opposite. I thought the promises she made of waiting to get married meant it would be something special. However it turned out to be a fundamental issue with her and she hated sex. Don't know why as she never shared her intimate internal feelings with me. Personally I think it had a lot to do with her dominating and bullying father with whom I never got on.

When Jenni was born in Peterborough hospital she came two weeks early mainly due I think to the Scottish party we were at two nights before. Elaine danced the Highland Fling, swinging around like a football in a tumble dryer. The baby had jaundice and was kept in an incubator for two weeks which definitely suppressed the bonding between mother and child. Elaine also had problems breast feeding. She didn't seem too good with pain and did not persevere.

I think today she would have been diagnosed with post natal depression but in those days the doctors just told her to pull herself together like they were talking to a pair of curtains.

I believe part of the problem had been the response of Elaine's father to the announcement of the pregnancy. He did not speak to her for about a month. Just shows how controlling and jealous he had become. Not a nice man at all which was not just my opinion.

I phoned my mum to tell her she was a Granny, her reaction was totally different. She boarded the first train out of Edinburgh and duly arrived in Peterborough to see the new Grandchild. When she arrived we went straight to the hospital only to be told she was not allowed in to the intensive care unit as the baby could only be attended by the parents. Despite her disappointment she was still overjoyed by the whole experience. What a wonderful, resilient woman she was and also very determined.

Jenni was born with red hair and was five pounds in weight. She cried a lot, in fact she cried all night for the first two years which put a tremendous strain on our marital relationship. I used to take Jenni out in the push chair at five and six in the morning just to relieve the situation. She also would work herself into such a state that her nose would bleed. Odd for a baby but that is just the way she was and she has turned out to be a fabulous mother herself. Jenni and I were, and are, very close.

While in Lincolnshire I behaved like Jack the Lad enjoying life as a young man should. I became social secretary of the local sports club and won the tennis singles trophy. I ran the discos and social events to make money for the club, including Strip nights for the men only. I hired two female strippers each time who would tease the audience with sexual performances. The pub we held it in was raided one of the nights and it was really quite comical to witness the clientele, including local county counsellors and off duty policemen, running out of the back door as the police came in the front.

While the girls and I sat in a corner of the pub to watch the ensuing   mayhem   unfold.

The girls of course now looked very respectable with all their clothes on and told me they were quite used to this happening in their profession.

It was quite comforting to know that if ever I wanted a favour the local councillors were more than happy to oblige when it came to planning permissions for the sports club.

All good things come to an end and when I had to resign from my job through inability to manage my life due to the drinking excessively.

Elaine's Uncle Ivan had found a shop up for sale in Edinburgh. We had a family consultation and Elaine's parents and mine put up the collateral to buy the business.

We moved into a flat above the shop, a fourth floor Victorian building with massive rooms including three bedrooms, a lounge, kitchen and bathroom. It was actually bigger than our house down in Market Deeping which was now up for sale.

Jenn
ifer and Arthur

Grannie Muriel Biggs and Grandpa Donald Biggs

SIXTEEN

Now I had found my ego again, I was a business man in
partnership with my wife, poor girl!
All went well to begin with, the clientele were supportive as it
had been family run affair and it seemed almost like having
an extended family.
Rising at five in the morning to prepare for the papers arriving
and get the seven boys and girls out on their rounds. To begin
with it was all new and exciting but after a while I felt
trapped. The children were two and four by this time and life
with a drunk was a challenge for my wife. She too was
unfulfilled and missed her professional standing. I imagine
she felt the same way in a fourth floor flat with two wee
bairns.
Before long I became agitated and looked for new ways to
amuse myself so I refurbished the shop completely from
something that looked akin to the shop on 'Open all hours', a
comedy program on TV, to a spanky new up to date store
where people could browse and choose. Obviously shop
lifting went up too but swings and round-abouts and all that!
However the turnover increased by more than fifty percent
and things were definitely looking up. Some of the locals still
hankered after the old shop but mostly people were very
positive.
My visits to the pub increased to every night after work
because I deserved it, or so I told myself. I would top it off at
home while having a social drink after offering my wife a
sherry. If she took it all the better, but if she did not she was

boring and trying to spoil my night after I had worked so hard to bring in the spoils of the day.

It was not long before the shop had a wee snifter tucked away in the corner of the store room, just so that I could relax when the door closed at six o'clock. Alcoholics like me do not honour our own promises as the lure of the bottle whispers 'just one more' before I put it away until tomorrow. A small drink turned into a quarter bottle and then a half, culminating in the purchase of a full bottle each and every day. The illness is very progressive and creates a delusional world in which I now was living.

But I was not an alcoholic because the morning drink had not yet appeared. However there is no defence against the progression and one morning an old lady presented me with the perfect justification for the morning 'hair of the dog'.

'Gosh' said the old lady 'you look rough on this cold winter morning'. 'Thanks' I said with a hint of sarcasm.

'I know what you need', continued the old dear, 'I take a wee brandy in my morning coffee to keep out the cold'.

Say no more I thought, bring out the bottle and from that moment I took a drop of the hard stuff in every coffee over the following two years. That equates to roughly two bottles of whisky each day and not even this devious and manipulative alcoholic can cover up that trail of wreckage.

By now I was fighting in the street with anybody that looked at me the wrong way. I was drunk behind the counter of the shop and not running the business properly.

I had great ideas of course. I decided the communal trees in our back green were in dire need of pruning. They were Oak and Chestnut trees all fully grown. So I hired a chain saw, borrowed a thirty foot ladder, drank a half bottle of whisky and swung from the upper branches like Tarzan in the jungle. I was having a great time whooping and laughing while those on the ground looked on like party poopers. I have got both legs and arms still attached to my body, all by the grace of God, whom I denied vehemently.

At this point in my life the family had a committee meeting and seemed to forget to ask me to attend. That could have a lot to do with the fact that the only item on the agenda was yours truly.

An ultimatum was issued which involved me attending the doctor's surgery with a view to being incarcerated in a mental hospital. I was so angry and full of resentment that these people could suggest that this honest, caring and hard-working individual could be treated so badly.

The upshot of it all was that I agreed to attend out patient's appointments every week for six months, which I thought had been quite a successful negotiation considering the size of the enemy forces.

It wasn't long before I turned the tables on them all by persuading the Psychiatrist that in fact my drink problem had been caused by the hard work, family pressures of young children and the never ending nagging and complaining of an ungrateful wife. All created in my own mind to protect whatever self-worth I had left which indeed was very little.

Five months of not drinking with the promise of a return to social drinking at the end, perfect.

I spent the following months proving to all and sundry that I was as normal as they were. Except for the alcohol consumption of course which was as abnormal as painting water surfaces. I attended many social functions where I pointed out the problem drinkers and criticised the drinking habits of my Wife, friends and relations. I hated the whole experience which prevented me from seeing that my life was improving dramatically both financially and mentally. Eventually it became like waiting for the holiday of a life time as the excitement built and I counted the days to the six month release from purgatory.

We had moved out of the flat into a lovely house with a garden. The business became successful again and we bought a new car. I appreciated all of these things but I could not see that the reason was abstinence from alcohol. The obsession still remained and the inevitable happened five and a half months after inception of my enforced sobriety. I went to the pub for a half of lager shandy. That is all it took to convince me I could handle my booze again. My wife showed bitter disappointment but I managed to convince her that her anxiety was unfounded. Life went on and my drinking increased secretly with a wee whisky here and there in-between apparently normal drinking habits.

Good neighbours, a much improved atmosphere and a chance to think straight provided the springboard for further thought about our circumstances. I worked seven days a week and found that I became genuinely tired after a day of work and there seemed little opportunity to have a family life as we all desired.

My wife and I kept our options open and soon found a business in the Scottish/English border country in a town called Wooler. The Borders are a beautiful part of the UK with rolling hills and long valleys and boasts the start of a walking trail named the Pennine Way.

The business we bought did not provide a service on Sundays and this looked an attractive proposition to develop our new found family life and a safe and tranquil atmosphere for our children to go to school.

We sold up in Edinburgh and moved to the Borders on the English side in Wooler, Northumberland.

GLENDALE ROAD WOOLER, SEVEN DOUBLED BEDROOMED MANSION, OWNWED FOR SEVEN YEARS.

SEVENTEEN
WOOLER, Northumberland.

We found a house that we both agreed on although it actually was my wife's choice as I favoured a bungalow that looked over the Glendale valley. However she won the day and we moved into this 150 year old, seven double bed roomed mansion. It could have housed an entire Salvation Army band and choir. Which would have been lovely at Christmas, but there was something too grandiose about the whole affair and after a few years the dream began to crumble.

At first of course, the excitement of the move, a new business and house kept us very busy.

However I had been naïve about the books and goodwill of the business. Margaret Thatcher the prime minister of the time was having a battle with the coal miners who owned all the caravans nearby. Unfortunately the miners lost their challenge and Maggy and her private army called the police force closed all the mines and virtually destroyed the North East of England in one fell swoop.

No miners, no caravan owners and no spare cash for the miner's families to spend in our shop.

Dear Mrs. Thatcher also hiked up the interest rates to 17.5% and the loan we had taken out to buy the business became an anchor around our necks so the business started to fail and the bills piled up and ultimately my drinking engulfed my very soul resulting in troubled relationships and financial ruin. We had to sell the house and buy a much smaller one.

During the rise and fall of the Biggs Empire my behaviour became erratic as I had ventured into the world of drinking and driving. God at this point had taken to looking after me. I would go to the pub in the car and completely forget that I had taken it there. The next morning I would wake up, look out the window and wonder where the car had gone. I even phoned the police to report it stolen only to be called by my friend the landlord of the Tankerville Arms wondering when I would be collecting my car from the car park. That was a blessing in disguise as I could not remember which pub I had gone to in the first place.

Now this is actually very relevant to the next episode when I looked out of the very same window a few weeks later to an empty street, no car. This time I had become wise to my behaviour and decided to go and look for the said vehicle. I did not have to venture far as I reached the bottom of the street to find my prized Cortina V6 poking out of the neighbour's hedge, doors wide open including the boot. There was nothing left in the car, no stereo radio and they had taken all my expensive fishing gear out of the boot compartment. I of course telephoned the police who were now quite used to my calls and said they would send someone round ASAP. Four hours later a constable arrived and virtually accused me of doing it myself whilst intoxicated. How could he think such a thing, I was mortified and carried that resentment against the coppers for years to come.

I later found out who had tried to take the car and the situation was handled out of court without the help of the police. All it needed was a baseball bat and a couple of pals. I had a certain reputation in the town as I ran the Karate club and taught all the hard boys in the area how to fight. It is not actually a great reputation to have as it comes with the challenges of all the wee wannabees in town looking for the top dog spot. All a bit tiresome really as it certainly was for my family.

That Cortina V6 had been my pride and joy as it was an X police car and went like shit off a shovel. It might have been fine if it had been driven by a sober person but when combined with alcohol it became a lethal weapon. So good in fact that one night a group of bank robbers targeted my car and stole it to do a post office robbery. I reported it stolen but you can imagine the response from the police. There wasn't much intervention until the car was found four days after the robbery, one hundred miles away in Gateshead near some high rise flats. I went down to collect the car only to find that they were still fingerprinting the vehicle for prints of the villains that had robbed the post office in Glanton, Northumberland. The other hiccup became evident when I tried to start the car. They had broken off the false key in the ignition and I could not ge5t the steering lock to disengage. Problem, however help was on hand as they say 'if you can't find the way ask a policeman'. I did just that as there were plenty about as you may have gathered. One of them produced a hammer and very larger screwdriver from his tool kit and proceeded to batter the lock in the steering column. It worked, the lock came off but the apparatus was now knackered completely but once again the policeman came to my rescue and said' just tell the insurance company that the villains did the damage. Job done!

The countryside around Wooler is quite stunning with the Cheviot Hills, country park land and it is just a skip and a hop to the coast where the beaches run for 90 miles or more with beautiful features like, Bamburgh Castle and the Holy Island where St Cuthbert practiced his ministry. Also nearby is the town of Berwick upon Tweed to the north which has changed hands from the English to the Scots and back innumerable times over the centuries of conflict between to two nations. To the south is the historical town of Alnwick which boasts one of the centres for Anglo/Scots conflict where Richard the Lion Heart defeated the Scots army in fields adjacent to the famous Castle, which gained further recognition in the 21st century as being one of the filming sites for the Harry Potter stories by J. K. Rowling.

Wooler itself was not devoid of fame with regards to the writing fraternity. John Conifer the author of Postman Pat children's story books based one of his characters on Mrs. Thompson, his wife's mother. She lived in Oliver Road and was a customer at the Corner Shop in the Market Square.

 This would be my shop, the new venture and reason for our family geographical to Wooler. I would be away from the ever more oppressive glare of our parents and Elaine's Uncle Ivan. He was a very nice and generous man but when it came to the business he became a predator in my everyday life. He meant well and looked after the interests of Elaine and her parents, but we both felt new surroundings and some independence would help our situation.

We transferred all the accounts into the Bank of Scotland (BOS), Wooler and made an appointment to see the new manager. Well I could not believe my luck when it turned out to be Larry Trainor, one of my old drinking buddies from the first branch I worked in at the British Linen Bank, Edinburgh. The old bank had been taken over by the BOS and his appointment was Wooler. What a spell of good luck for me and bad luck for my wife and family as we paired up in the pool team, playing for Tankerville Arms Hotel in the local league.

My drinking started as purely social, or so I thought at the time. The progression of the illness is cunning and baffling but the one certainty is that it does progress.

After my enforced sobriety at the hands of the mental health services I had no intention to return to the miseries of the previous years.

In fact one of the characteristics of my drinking was to avoid becoming drunk at all costs. I have always feared the 'whirly pits' of intoxication, the inevitable vomiting and the humiliation.

Larry and I became firm drinking buddies, along with many other 'Dolerites' such as, Big Jim the owner of the Red Lion, Big Soup my pool partner, and the list goes on. Wooler was, and still is, a den of iniquity, with regards to drugs and alcohol.

It also had a reputation for one of the highest rates of paedophilia recorded in the country. Numerous cases went to court, resulting in successful prosecution of family members abusing their children and grandchildren.

That sort of sums up Wooler with regard to some of the inhabitants, however there is the up side, the beautiful countryside and the decent people who cherished and loved their children giving them an education based on a rural setting. The schools were of a good standard and the educational results of my children reflect the teaching standards. Both did very well although Jonathan stumbled into bad company which halted his progress in the academic sense, he definitely takes after me. But Jennifer was a very dedicated student achieving a degree in psychology and later went on to become a teacher like her mother.

So here we are in Wooler. The kids are in the local first school. My wife and I are partners in a business. We have a big seven double bedroom house. Old friends reunited in the form of the bank manager and his family. I had everything to live for except I had not changed, I was still the same wee boy inside with very little self worth. My remedy remained the same, creating false identity through individual acts which boosted my ego enough to feel some self respect.

Whilst in Edinburgh I took up Karate to find self respect after I was discharged from the Royal Edinburgh Mental Hospital. They thought and I believed that my problems were solved but the services did not carry any form of follow up treatment or support. I therefore reverted to previous beliefs and behaviour, weaning myself back onto the bottle. This disease is truly baffling, powerful and progressive.

I loved learning Shotokan Karate and discipline behind the spiritual essence of the martial art.

My sensei was a Japanese man called Mr. Tomita who was six feet four and built like a proverbial brick toilet. Hard as nails, very supple and moved like a well oiled machine. He also drank bottles of vodka on a regular basis which was definitely something to emulate. Of course this was another great excuse to consume my favourite poison while learning how to defend myself under the instruction of a 6th Dan master of the art.

At first it would only be a quickie after work to relax me and give me the confidence to face the hard training regime and pain of a three hour session in the Dojo.

As it turned out I found that I had a natural ability and joined the fighting team as the anchor man. This was the name given to the last man to fight and it is especially important that it should be someone they felt would have a good chance of winning as it meant the score of the contest was even. I was good at fighting and really quite aggressive. If only they knew it had come from a fear of losing or being hurt. Maybe they did, I will never know.

So when I moved to Wooler there was no club to attend. I gave myself a promotion in order to start the club. I went from white belt to green and became the Sensei of the Tora Kita Shotokan club in Wooler. We had a visit one night from the nearby Alnwick club who asked me if my club would like to affiliate with them. I of course said 'yes' and we instantly had two black belts as our instructors. I progressed through he belts, legitimately this time to first Kya brown belt.

My drinking was at first only a couple before I went to the club for 'Dutch courage' but eventually progressed to the point that I could not even practice the one thing that had been building my self confidence. ALCOHOLISM IS INDEED CUNNING, BAFFLING AND POWERFUL.

The club at first had upwards of fifty members from the age of seven to seventy. Many of them did drift away as it is a very hard sport and requires some dedication to keep up the fitness and standard necessary to participate.

We went out running in the ice and snow in bare feet, even the little ones. My instruction seemed to be of a high standard as many of the students became brown belts themselves. The club was asked to do a demonstration once at the local Fete day and we practiced for weeks to get it right. Unfortunately I was in one of my worst fazes of alcoholism and I had to hand over the job of leading it to one of my students claiming I was suffering from an illness. I did not realise how right I was about the 'illness' part.

During this period of my life I have a lot of blanks, blackouts they call them in Alcoholics Anonymous. I functioned at work and at home but the details are very vague and sketchy. My family suffered greatly during this time and a lot of my amends relate to my behaviour towards family, friends, relations and especially my wife Elaine and children, Jennifer and Jonathan. To them I owe a debt of gratitude for their love and resilience through unbelievable hardship.

The business I bought had two staff and a regular clientele which judging from the accounts would give us a reasonable standard of living so the future looked rosy. However within a short space of time, Margaret Thatcher the Prime Minister was at odds with the miners union. The miners all had caravans around Wooler and were a major part of our summer turn over. The consequence of this dispute reduced the spending power of the miners and their families and hence the business suffered so we reduced the staff to one. Next came a hike in the interest rates to a dizzy level of 17.5%. Our mortgage and business bank loan became untenable so we had to sell the big house and buy a smaller three bed detached round the corner.

My drinking worsened and so did my mood. To add to the troubles my Father died in London which must be one of the worst exhibitions of my alcoholic behaviour during my illness. I promised my Father I would give up the drink while sitting by his bed as he was dying. All I could feel was self pity and poor me. Without a thought for the pain my Mother went through or my sister or children. Another example of the amends I would later have to make in my recovery.

The business went under and Elaine had to return to teaching which actually must have been a relief for her as she could escape my control and regain her self-worth.

I struggled to get employment but the kindness of friends gave me a job on a couple of farms. The first was an organic farm where I dipped sheep, bailed hay and painted barns with creosote.

My financial recompense for the employment worked out at three pounds fifty per hour, a pauper's wage but needs must as I was at the low ebb of my earning powers.

This time in my life should have taught me loads about humility but the grandiose alcoholic in me was still present along with a bottle of Vodka every day which accounted for at least fifty percent of the wages. I still talked myself up telling everyone of my great deeds in the financial world and the poor me syndrome which blamed the whole situation on Maggy Thatcher and greed of the banking system. Not of course entirely untrue but I have since learned through the program of Alcoholics Anonymous that blame is one of the blocks to spiritual development.

My whole experience of the nineteen eighties is a blur of blackouts and humiliation creating countless opportunities for steps eight and nine of the AA program to make amends where ever possible except when to do so would injure others, reflected in the chapter on relationships, which might have been better entitled Affairs of the Penis.

I gave up so many of the things that gave me a passion for life during my drunken days in Wooler.

I struggled to perform Karate so I gave it up rather than stop drinking. I gave up golf rather than put down the bottle. I made a fool of myself playing tennis, my most favourite sport at which I would have excelled if not for my need for inebriation. Worst of all I sacrificed my family, friends and tragically my self-worth and spiritual well being with the compulsion intoxication.

I developed a devious, manipulative and dishonest character in order to enable lack of choice over the King Alcohol.

EIGHTEEN

I am a naturally sensitive person who felt enormous guilt through lying to my loved ones about my drinking. I felt crushing remorse about my failure to succeed in any of my choices of career.

The only solution for these crippling feelings resulted in further emersion into the illness of alcoholism. The final conclusion to my journey drove me into desperation and frequent attempts at suicide and self destruction. I wished for the end as no human power seemed to solve my Alcoholism.

I attended the GP surgery on numerous occasions hoping that I could have a proper illness, one that others recognised, and something that would give me attention and pity from my family and piers.

I dreamt of contracting Cancer and or a heart attack. I fantasised about plans for my own funeral and how everybody would be so sad and sorry that they did not understand poor Arthur.

In 1984 I was diagnosed as having a Myocardial Infarction after the severest of pains in my chest. I went for blood tests, treadmill and angiogram examinations. I was advised about my diet and warned about my alcohol consumption so I stopped drinking for a couple of weeks to prove to myself and my family that the drinking had no part in my problem.

I had become truly insane but I and my family had six more years of this purgatory to endure before the final episode in 1989 when the final suicide attempt was all but successful.

This accounts for one of the most significant spiritual experiences on my journey.

I said goodbye to my wife at the front door as she departed for a shopping trip to the local main street. It was nine in the morning. As soon as she turned the corner I made the usual 'B' line for the garage where my stash of Vodka lay in wait of my arrival. With a sigh of relief I opened the bottle and poured a half dozen finger measure into a glass, lifting it to my face with mouth watering anticipation.

At that moment the garage door opened and there stood my wife looking aghast at the apparition that met her gaze. Her husband standing there, glass in hand, mouth open and head cocked to receive the first of the day's medicine.

'What's that', she said, and I replied, 'vodka'?

I never usually told the truth but this time the words just popped out. There seemed no defence, no alternative, I was devastated, just as she was to find me there glass in hand. Something inside me snapped and I drank the whole bottle down after she walked away.

I went into the house and swallowed every pill I could find including Paracetamol, Aspirin and a bucket load of anti-depressants the doctor had prescribed, and lay down on the bed to die.

I have no recollection of what happened in the world around me but I had a clear and conscious experience of darkness and felt myself floating towards something as I lay dying. Within this experience I found myself being pushed back by what seemed like a hand. It seemed a very conscious moment even though I was in essence physically dead with no heart beat and I had ceased breathing according to my wife who found me in the bedroom.

She explained that the room had been covered in blood and I lay prostrate on the floor. She told me later that she thanked God that it was all over and she would not have to contend with my behaviour any longer.

Elaine, at the age of sixteen had been a caring, lovely person with whom I had fallen in love. This illness gradually stripped away her-self worth, confidence and spiritual well being. Alcoholism is so powerful it takes away rational choice and human dignity.

To the this day of writing I have always loved her and would love to make amends but I have done so much damage to a wonderful, happy and bubbling person that I feel there may be no alternative but to accept the pain I feel at our separation in 1993.

This incident happened in the summer of 1989 but it was not until the 4th of November that my higher power decided that I had had enough pain and had reached my final spiritual rock bottom.

At the time of these episodes I had taken a part time job driving school buses in the morning and evening, which was less than ideal but employment in rural Northumberland was fairly sparse.

I had promised the Doctor, Noel Roy that I would not drink or let it affect my driving in any way so he signed the forms for my PSV licence to drive buses.

I am moderately pleased to say that I kept that promise but the intervals between driving became islands of intoxication as the illness progressed. I would stop drinking on the Sunday, shaking and feeling like vomiting all day in order to sober up for the driving on a Monday morning. I would last all week without a drink but hated every moment of this enforced sobriety. The promise of a bottle of Vodka on a Friday night kept me focused all wee. I was so obsessed by the promise of a drink that I could not see that the period between drinks made my life easier and my family happier. The family all dreaded Friday nights where I embraced alcohol like a long lost friend. Somewhere in my psyche I also started to enjoy the withdrawals on Sunday and Monday in order to get the excitement of the promise of the next drink. I believe the insanity of alcoholism had finally taken a major step towards my spiritual degradation.

This is the point in my journey through life where my career and personal wellbeing took a life changing turn about.

NINETEEN
Like a new born, up and running!

I spent the first 14 years of my life as a people pleasing individual with very little self worth, followed by the consumption of alcohol for 25 years, progressing into active alcoholism in the final stages.

In contrast, I can visualise my new found sobriety as a new born animal staggering to find their feet after being introduced to a brand new world. Everything I experienced was seen from a new perspective.

No longer did I have to deny that I had had a drink when quizzed by my family or friends. No longer did I have to get up in the morning and question whether I had any left over from the night before. No longer did I have to manage my purchase of alcohol, deciding which shop to buy it from in order to avoid any questions about my consumption. There was also the breath taking (literally) reality that I could function physically, mentally and spiritually. No withdrawals or 'hangovers' as we call them.

The list is really endless and the joys of feeling, smelling, hearing and seeing everything around me was quite overpowering in a liberating and spiritual way.

Physically the first few weeks of sobriety were difficult although in a way amusing. I would open a door and walk into the side of it before it was fully open, ouch! I would try to run up the stairs and catch my feet on the step with a resultant thud as I hit the ground and bruised knees. Very dangerous this sobriety but well worth the pain.

The worst experience came in the form of a bus crash. Yep, no half measures for me, just the true reality of misjudgement, only an inch or two but, a mistake just the same.

I used to drink to forget the emotional pain of such episodes. Any excuse created the justification sufficient to placate my remorse and embarrassment.

My job required me to drive a bus for Northumberland Motor Company, mostly school runs but some town work when they were short of drivers. I caught the tail end of a parked car with the back wheel arch of the bus. I wrote off three cars, one which was owned by the local elder of the church I was about to attend, although I did not know this at the time. He also had the prestigious job of maintaining the town clock on top of the church tower in Wooler. Actually he just wound it up and set the time when it ran slow, which kept him busy nearly every day.

The senses began to return in a vibrant manner. I heard the morning chorus from the birds without covering my head and looking for a shot gun to avoid the happiness of a brand new day. There had been no pleasure in the morning until the first drink reached it's target.

Food became a pleasure rather than a necessity as my taste buds recovered from the constant onslaught of Alcohol. No more sweating out the Vodka.

Reactions became quite hyper sensitive which is a joy to experience after the initial misguided incidents.

The relief of not drinking is quite astonishing. The panic of being found out was taken away. Which is a myth in the mind of the addict anyway, as everyone knows what is going on, but they are too scared to confront the drinker for the fear of being lied to again and again.

TWENTY
Introduction to the Program

At seven o'clock in the evening of 5th November 1989 I finally got a human being to answer the telephone helpline of Alcoholics Anonymous.

The guy at the other end of the line asked if he could help and I proceeded to tell him I had a problem with alcohol and that my concern was that I could not stay away from the first drink for any significant period of time. I had stopped on many hundreds of occasions but always returned to the bottle when I felt I had gained enough control of my personal life. When my friends and family had backed off and begun to accept me back into the fold. This once lasted for the lengthy period of five
months at the age of twenty nine but in all that time of abstemious austerity I had one thought in my mind and that was how to return to my magic alexia, the cure for all my emotional, spiritual and physical ails.

After several minutes of total verbal bollocks he waited to hear if I had finished, and then patiently, calmly and serenely told me he thought I sounded ready for Alcoholics Anonymous and proceeded to give me the number of someone to call who may be able to help me.

I felt like the first time in all my life I had been accepted for myself without argument, comment or judgement. It seemed like total non conditional acceptance and that must have been what I was looking for in all the previous attempts at asking for help.

The seed was sown, I became hooked into the promise of sobriety especially after the next two phone calls I made to other existing members of the fellowship.

On the Tuesday of the same week a gentleman came to my house in Wooler and shared his personal story with me. I now know this selfless action to be called 'twelfth stepping'.

He invited me to come to an AA meeting in Morpeth, which I deemed to be fairly safe as it was far enough away from prying eyes. After all I could not let people think I might be a drunk now could I.!!!

I find it amazing in the light of sobriety how we can be ashamed of trying to solve our drink problem. If we are drunk in the street we just don't care but if someone saw us getting sober we are the opposite.

I could not accompany him to the meeting until the following Monday night as I was too busy. He must have thought I was a proper waste of time but he waited and I called him the next week to say I would be there but only if he would be there too. I was too scared to go on my own.

Monday the 20th November 1989 may possibly be the most important day of my whole life as I entered the rooms of the Methodist Church, Morpeth for my first Alcoholics Anonymous meeting.

It is probably the only decision in my life about which I have had no second thoughts. No regrets, nor indecision, I will always be forever grateful for the unconditional welcome I received that night, by complete strangers who had all been through hell and back. All they required from me was to have a desire to stop drinking and to this day of writing I have been given the keys of the kingdom of heaven, contentment and an inner peace which is surpassed by nothing else in my life I have ever experienced.

There were six people around the table, men and women from all walks of life all with a desire to stay away from a drink one day at a time.

I was offered a cup of tea and a biscuit and told to listen for the similarities, not the differences. I could speak if I wanted or just listen if I felt more comfortable with that.

One by one they shared their stories of oblivion through alcohol, black outs where they functioned but had no recollection of what they had done. They sacrificed the love of their family for the sake of a drink. They lied to themselves and others about their condition. They called their condition an illness of denial.

I identified with almost everything they said and realised we all had a different pathway but ended up in the same emotional prison and spiritual degradation.

The group spoke of their belief in a Higher Power, the fellowship with a common purpose to stay away from the first drink, the 12 step program, a Sponsor and a desire to change. All of these things seemed attractive to me and for that I am grateful as it has given me 25 years of continuous sobriety.

TWENTY ONE
SOBRIETY THE FIRST 42 MONTHS

It is advised in the world of AA never to make any major decisions in the first two years, because it takes that period of time to re-establish some modicum of sanity.

If an Alcoholic knew how intensely difficult the emotional transition of sobriety would be, I cannot imagine that any of us would even entertain the possibility of long term recovery. There is no doubt in my mind that Human Beings are blessed that we cannot predict the future.

It is also a blessing that the vision of the founders of AA believed that we can only live one day at a time.

Withdrawals from Alcohol require the system to balance itself chemically. I had spent the last twenty five years changing the chemistry of all the nervous, endocrine, circulatory, digestive and respiratory systems in my body from one of normality to alcohol dependency.

This is common sense to any normal individual, but an Alcoholic replaces common sense with self will run riot.

It took at least a month for the physical, mechanical workings of my body to reprogram itself and accept it was no longer being run on ether alcohol. The muscular pain from cramping was hard to endure but the communication system from my brain function, through the nervous system to my mechanical motion took the longest to balance out.

The coordination and judgement faltered on many occasions culminating in various accidents with doors, stairs and more seriously writing off the three cars with the bus.

However these things did stop eventually, with the daily intake of proper vitamins, carbohydrates, and nutrients necessary for the body to produce balanced food for my brain cells. If there were any left to feed!

My frame of mind improved due to the positive regard I experienced from the fellowship of AA. I began to learn about sober relationships with other people without the fear of inadequacy. This in turn enabled my self-worth to grow.

When attending an AA meeting for the first time I experienced an unconditional positive regard from everybody in the room. There was only one requirement for membership and that was a desire to stop drinking and the willingness to stay stopped.

The shares around the room were so honest and selfless. Not like the old days of standing at the bar trying to outdo your neighbour in order to bolster one's own ego.

These AA stories were believable told with a degree of humility I had never found in any drinking establishment.

After I went home full of hope for the first time in a decade all I wanted to do was share it with my family and friends. Unfortunately those who have been around a practicing alcoholic have learned to distrust anything they say due to the false promises and broken agreements of the past.

When someone joins AA they are on their own apart from these new found friends who are all recovering alcoholics. Trust has to be earned back from our families and that can take years of altered behaviour and sometimes as in my case my Wife was never able to regain her original trusting nature where I was concerned. This led to a divorce ultimately with emotional breakdowns for us both.

There is no comfort in the fact that a large percentage of marriages fail when recovery enters the relationship. This is a very serious family illness with a very complex structure. Initially recovery demands a great deal of dedication on behalf of the Addict/Alcoholic. One hundred percent of our energy has to be directed to find a solution for the emptiness left by the void of abstinence. After a few weeks of sobriety I was coming to believe that I had found a solution. I began to want my family back. I wanted to repair the relationship with my wife and children, family and friends. I no longer felt alone with that awful ache in my heart that I would never make a return to the normal world. I knew I felt and thought differently but no one can see inside my head so all I could give were assurances that this time everything had changed. I learned that it can be impossible to convince anyone who has experienced the consistent promises of false hope issued by an Alcoholic or drug addict.

It is a myth that AA gets us sober, it doesn't, that is a decision we make ourselves. But when we combine that decision with a fellowship of like minded people who have experienced the pains of our dishonesty, manipulation and devious behaviour, then we have a chance. If we couple this with a desire to stop drinking, followed by a specially designed program for misfits like us, the 12 steps of the AA program, then we have a solution.

It is all about treating the physical, mental and spiritual aspects of Alcoholism at the same time, through one non restrictive medium.

There is little doubt that I became hooked on the recovery program of AA and handed my life and soul over to the care of this new found Higher Power.

Gradually I became interested in my family again and had a deep desire to fix the broken relationship with my wife, Elaine, but I would to find out through extreme pain and anguish, some things are beyond sticky tape.

TWENTY TWO

I was born into a Christian or family and introduced to Christian morals and fellowship at an early age through Sunday school while my Mum attended church.

I was a super sensitive wee boy. I could not handle emotions of conflict or a criticism and consequently developed negative feelings of inadequacy.

Nothing seemed to relieve my anxiety about life. I just did not feel good enough or that I fitted in.

My spiritual identity drifted into people pleasing.

However at 14 I did find a temporary solution in the form of a magic chemical Alexia called Alcohol. My troubles just disappeared, suppressed by the utopia of this mind altering chemical. I felt at ease. I had found the easier softer way. However, 10 years passed by and the solution was turning into a problem.

This artificial higher power, now my solution for all aspects of my life became a problem for my family friends. They tried to take away my higher power, working on my feelings of guilt and remorse which were born from the denial of a true God in my life. I believe that this was the conception of my spiritual illness. My consumption increased as my self-worth deteriorated. I became dishonest with myself and others about the depth of my problem. As a consequence I became isolated from their love and affection as I rejected them in preference to a bottle of booze. I handed my life and my will over to the alcohol. I gave my loved ones false promises. I also demanded gods help but he was not listening! Or a so I thought!

As my life became unmanageable no human power could relieve my alcoholism. I tried doctors psychiatrists and clergymen none of them worked.

My daily life now had become a desperate attempt at accessing normality, to be like the other human beings that surrounded my everyday existence. I felt like someone in a prison cell looking out through the bars and wondering if I could ever be like them, if I would ever find true happiness. I was terrified to join them in fear of not matching up to their, or especially my own, expectations.

It is a very lonely place at to be at the end of one's spiritual wellbeing. But I do believe that this is the only road to recovery. The barrel needs to be completely empty before introducing fresh apples.

Having reached this point on the 4th November 1989 I became open to a spiritual intervention. I cannot describe how I felt as I felt nothing at all. Open mindedness and a feeling that I was at last ready and willing to honestly face my illness became my greatest asset. Surrender, which had never been an option for this stubborn alcoholic, would soon turn my weakness into strength.

For years I had tested God, demanding divine intervention and feeling that it had always eluded me. Therefore this had been my proof against the existence of any higher power. I felt unloved and abandoned. Alone on a stormy sea, where prayer seemed fruitless until I asked that God would take me from this purgatory as I had had enough and there was no hope left in my life.

On the 5th of November 1989 I found the courage to call the Alcoholics Anonymous helpline. It was answered by a man called 'Irish John' who gave me hope and understanding I had not experienced from any other human being.

I spent the next 18 months becoming part of the fellowship of AA. Using the Serenity Prayer as a mantra when I felt overwhelmed by the pressures of sobriety and each day's general problems.

TWENTY THREE

The program of AA requires the individual to form a belief in a Higher Power. All of the steps to recovery are of a spiritual nature. Anyone coming in to AA has used Alcohol as their solution to their life problem, therefore it has to be replaced by an alternative solution. A belief that Alcohol is the only answer to the pains of everyday existence has to be replaced by something else or a return to the consumption of the mind altering chemical will be inevitable.

So the first step deals with the problem, I am powerless over alcohol and every time I consume it, it sets off a compulsion to follow it up with a second blast causing the problem. The obsession in the mind becomes too hard and painful to deny. I have heard it said that the addict is devoid of will power. This is totally untrue as it takes severe will power to drink through the pain of addiction.

The second step of the AA program deals with the solution which asks and requires a complete change of thinking, behaviour and attitude. For this we addicts need guidelines in a program set out to analyse our personality disorder and correct the defects of character.

So a spiritual change needs a spiritual program and that is exactly what the 12 steps are designed for in AA.

A sudden decision to believe in a God is a difficult scenario for a self-willed alcoholic. Therefore a gradual change of heart will be the best solution. Proof of change is also an encouraging prospect as addicts are naturally cautious or even distrusting of other people's motives for helping.

How does one start to believe in a power greater than oneself?

I believe in electricity but I cannot see it, I can only feel it if I stick my finger in the wrong place.

I believe in air to keep me alive because if I stop inhaling it, I die and it feels very uncomfortable while refraining from breathing.

I believe in physical pain before it happens because I have hurt in the past, so I work hard to avoid it.

I will go to any lengths to access treatment when a physical pain becomes too intense to suffer it any longer.

I will seek a solution to any uncomfortable feelings of mental anguish because I know that there is a chemical or psychological cure.

I accept that physical and mental conditions exist even when I cannot see or feel them in the material world.

Spiritual belief appears to be totally different and very much more difficult for many people. There are so many channels to choose from to access a Higher Power or indeed for those who wish to deny the existence of any greater being or entity.

I myself have swung from one belief to another but never really denied the existence of a God in my life, but I have struggled to identify a specific source for my focus.

'Identify yourself now and all shall be well', everyone will finally be able to remove all doubt and we can bow down to the ultimate source of power and energy. That unfortunately will never happen for Humans as we are all doubters of the truth, even the whole truth.

One day after 18 months of sobriety I made a spur of the
moment decision to enter the Church of England in Wooler.
No reason, I just felt like it when dropping of my wife, Elaine,
on Sunday morning for her weekly pilgrimage to St Mary's
church.

I went in and felt welcomed and by the time I had sat through
the service I decided I would like to try this new founds
salvation again. No big deal, it was just a decision.

For the next two years I became a part of this ritual and
enjoyed the experience. I joined the church music group and
we played in churches across Northumberland. I gathered
with new found friends to pray and discover our motivation
for life and develop our personal life skills.

Life started to mean something special and I was asked to
present the 'Time for Thought' on Radio Borders. Pupils at my
children's school started to ask if their Dad was a Vicar. The
answer of course should have been 'No, he is just an X-drunk
who's ego is surpassing all expectations.'

That is maybe a little unfair to me as it is only a small part of
my journey in the spiritual realm. I did however stray from
the path of the straight and narrow after three and a half
years of sobriety. A path I regret today as it led me away from
my loving family and destroyed the life I was building in
sobriety.

On the other hand I met and eventually married again to
enjoy a further 18 years with a very special person who
unfortunately turned against me and treated me with
complete disrespect. But this also led me to where I am today
with a commitment to become a Christian Soldier journey

with the Salvation Army. I am really happy with this new found decision to hand my life and will over to the care of God through the Son of God, Jesus Christ.

AFFAIRS OF THE HEART
TWENTY FOUR

I had many affairs of the heart and body during my years as a practicing Alcoholic. I am not proud of my behaviour but the only thing Elaine and I did not share was a demonstrative nature. She hated sex and I loved it. Neither do I regret the encounters as the women in question were all very special parts of my life and I loved them all which tore me apart as I also truly believe that Elaine always was and always will be the most special of them all.

My first affair happened when I moved with Polydor Record Company to the south east of England.

I went on my own at first as Elaine had a job in the Scottish border town of Kelso as a teacher. It was a year after we were married and our sexual incompatibility began to rear its ugly head.

I met a beautiful young lady called Mandy who took me hostage as her lover and I loved every minute of her company. Now she definitely fulfilled my needs as a demonstrative person and we had a very vibrant sexual encounter each time we met illicitly.

Then the inevitable happened and she fell pregnant. She gave birth to a wee boy that she named Christopher whom I met only twice, once when she gave birth to him in Stamford hospital and again a year later when I visited them both while on holiday with Elaine in Market Deeping where we had lived for three years. Mandy choose to be a single Mother and was adamant that she would bring up the child as her son and did not want a man in her life.

She never to this day told me I was the Father and I have never seen them since that last visit in 1976. He is the same age as Jennifer, my daughter, who was born in Peterborough Hospital.

While I am in a confession mode I may as well write about my other infidelities.

The first which I have recounted in the sketchy detail, more for the preservation of the reputation of the Mistress rather than the Adulterer, happened in the mid seventies and continued for about a year.

The second encounter transpired in Edinburgh, my home city. In the 1970's I played in a band with a following of some very beautiful young girls, one of whom went by the name of Elizabeth, Libby to her friends. She was very pleasing on the eye with long black hair and attractive features. We had a few intimate nights together while my girlfriend, Elaine (destined to be my unfortunate wife some years later), worked up in the north of Scotland as a teacher.

Libby and I had always been friends and would be today if we ever met up. She became a theatre sister in an Edinburgh hospital as she was a very bright young lady with a determination to be admired.

In the nineteen eighties I used to travel to Edinburgh to watch the international rugby at Murrayfield. After the game I met up with all my old pals one of which was Libby. One thing I have omitted to explain is that Libby was one of my wife Elaine's best friends from school. The evening progressed as usual from drinks at all the pubs around Rose Street in the city centre to a party at someone's house.

Libby and I just seemed to melt together and ended up in her flat for the night all under Libby's control with my more than willing participation. I got in the In-law's bad books as I was supposed to be spending the night at their house, so I ended up using some very lame excuses for my absence, saying I was too drunk to drive home which was probably one hundred per cent accurate.

I have to say I worried about the consequences of ever being found out for a very long time after the event.

The penultimate affair while married to Elaine developed from my egotistic opinion of myself as a Karate teacher in Wooler. One of the children had a particularly attractive mother and I fell for her attentions at the drop of a hat, actually it was the drop of another garment that sealed the deal while Elaine visited her mother in Edinburgh. Shirley happened to be an extremely active nymphomaniac when it came to our liaison. She was literally the answer to my dreams as I had fantasised about meeting someone like her for years. Be careful what you pray for I always say because one day you might just get it.

We met regularly for four years usually on the Karate nights and always when Elaine went away on her jaunts to Edinburgh or her sister in Shropshire. In my defence I was a practicing Alcoholic at the time but really there is no excuse for infidelity, or is there?

Unfortunately when a relationship goes beyond a couple of encounters it can become more serious for one or both of the participants. In this case Shirley apparently had fallen in love with me. I was very fond of her but there were no deep feelings of love on my part. Not enough to leave my family as I doted on my children and always have done, that is true unconditional love.

I remember one occasion when Elaine had gone away for a wee holiday with the kids. She left a note under my pillow which had the message 'I love you'' written out with a heart drawn on it. I knew nothing about this note, until, having spent the night with Shirley in my bed, I returned home after work to find a note from Shirley, who had gone home by now, written on the back of Elaine's note saying she loved me too. Now I was in a mess, not only did Shirley think I loved her but it was in response to Elaine devoting her love which to be honest was a rare event. Not surprising really considering my alcoholic behaviour over the years of our marriage.

Shirley and I had a good relationship up until she informed me one night that she had not been around for a while as she had fallen pregnant and without telling me she had gone to Edinburgh for an abortion. I was actually quite devastated as I have never agreed with abortion unless it is for good medical or psychological reasons.

I had to make a decision between one or the other and quite frankly there was no contest as I did love Elaine and the children and always had done, but our sexual incompatibility as man and wife became a problem for me as I am probably the male equivalent of a nymphomaniac.

So the scene was set for the final night of promiscuity between Shirley and me.

I went to her cottage as usual after Karate club and ended up in bed with her which was not my intention but when the urge called I could not resist the temptation. Unfair I know as I had decided to tell her I could not carry on with the deceit and would not see her again.

I thought that I had handled the termination of our relationship quite sensitively but Shirley had a completely different view of my honourable intentions to spend the rest of my life with my family.

I returned home, leaving Shirley in tears, and breathed a sigh of relief that I was free from my own adulterous behaviour. All was well until 3am, when the telephone rang waking Elaine and me from our slumber. I went to answer the call only to hear Shirley on the other end telling me what she thought of me and that I had better watch my back as she would blow me away with her ex husband's shotgun then the line went dead. I worried for months after the call which I imagine was her intention all along. Well done Shirley, I deserved every moment of having to look over my shoulder and at every passing car which looked like hers.

There are two more indiscretions in my affairs of the heart, although I think another part of the anatomy slightly further south of the heart played a big part in the events that followed my first four years of sobriety.

ALCOHOLICS ANONYMOUS
TWENTY FIVE

AA became a very major part of my life through absolute necessity or I would have reverted to the illness without a doubt. I need a program in my life that helps me adjust my natural desires into a balanced format. Changing is a very insecure prospect for a recovering Alcoholic, but one that is absolutely essential. That is why we need help from a Sponsor that has already been through the process, the 12 step program, the fellowship and sharing of like minded people and the part that most people struggle with, a Higher Power, the one I call God.

Elaine attended Al-Anon, the sister fellowship to AA for the support of the family and partners. At first she found this fellowship helpful but as time went by and I started to live my life without the influence of alcohol she drifted away from the support network which in hindsight became a problem as it is impossible to return to the previous normality if there ever was any!

There were really happy times for me in those four years. I became a proper Father to Jenni and Jonathan, going on holidays with them and enjoying their company.

We went to Loch Carron every year with Elaine's uncle and cousins and stayed in a beautiful mansion called Little Kelso, which was owned by the late Lord Montgomery, the one who was blown up in his yacht by the IRA.

We also had a fantastic trip to France where we stayed in Le Thillot at a wee resort with tennis courts and a pool. These happy memories were a new experience for me, along with the jaunts in the caravan to Yorkshire, where we played daft games in the fields where we camped. All good family fun and they seem to be the holidays that my children remember the most, the simple life.

I worked for the bus company during this time, running school kids back and forwards in the mornings and afternoons. Sometimes it was a fabulous job, but more often an occupation from hell with the behaviour of the kids on the bus.

After a while the challenge of this occupation dragged its heels and I became discontent, looking for new horizons and more job satisfaction, in fact I was bored, and that is dangerous for a recovering addict.

I reached the magic age of forty in early sobriety and so did Elaine. She was born one month after me in 1950, on the 12th of May. We arranged a joint party to celebrate in the middle of the Cheviot hills in a place called College Valley which is infamous for its hunting dogs and precocious idiots that chase around after them murdering foxes for personal entertainment.

However the venue suited both of us for the party as we wanted to have a live band and about 150 guests to celebrate our middle aged rebellion. I had been sober for six months, so it was a massive step for me to be part of the limelight. During my years of alcoholism my ego searched for attention as the King of the Castle. That comes at a price when you don't have any courage or self-worth, and I had no self-worth because I had no courage. I feared not being good enough and had a terror of making any mistakes.

Add alcohol and all of these character defects disappear instantly. Job done, the easier softer way to mature, playing the part of an adult, or so I thought.

But not in these days of sobriety, I prayed for the courage to behave and act like an adult and it worked. I made a speech in front of all our guests whilst shaking and sweating with fear, but I managed to complete the task which was one of the first tastes of the joys of being sober.

I continued to go to AA and began to do service. I chaired meetings, helped look after the finances, did secretarial duties, I joined the Intergroup which looked after the interests of all the local groups in the area. I loved the responsibility supported by a Sponsor who guided me in the program helping me to become the person I was always meant to be.

TWENTY SIX
THE END OF FAMILY LIFE

There were several signs however, that Elaine had little understanding of my needs in sobriety. I tried genuinely to make amends for my previous behaviour while drinking but there were some situations she could not seem to find the ability to trust me and others where she expected me to be 'Normal', whatever that is!

I don't think she would ever have been able to change and because of this our relationship broke down as I changed radically. I think in a positive way, but once she asked for the old Arthur back but without the drink. That did not make any sense to me or probably for any rational thinking human being.

I did make a few decisions that were less than sensitive to Elaine's feelings and I am not proud of them but they did change my life completely, allowing me to develop emotionally. It is always painful to grow in a spiritual way and we both suffered a very painful break up of our twenty year marriage.

I will not go into infinite detail but this is a brief resume of my insensitive approaches to sorting out our differences, bearing in mind that Elaine must have been in an emotional turmoil through suffering from my Alcoholism and the fact that she had cast aside Al Anon thinking everything would go back to how it was in the past, but without Alcohol of course.

I broached the subject of our marriage when I took her out on our twentieth anniversary. I asked if we could talk about our relationship as I wanted to be happy with her.

This obviously was taken out of context as she asked why I was unhappy. I said I was not unhappy but wanted to sort out any differences we might have since I got sober.

I have to say what came next was like a bolt of lightning hitting my sensitive parts. Right said she, let's get divorced. Wait a minute I thought this is not going in the direction of reconciliation.

At this point I think she had grasped an opportunity to come out with something that had been on her mind for some time.

She never backed down after that night despite my repeated approaches and attempts to back-peddle and start again.

I never wanted to lose my family and still today regret what happened and how vicious it became as her friends became involved giving her support and telling her what she wanted to hear, that none of this was her fault and she would be better off without me. In particular her sister who wrote me an unforgivable letter telling me how I had sponged all our married life and many more hurtful and quite untrue statements.

The actual split happened at 4am in the morning. I had collected Jenni from her night out in Alnwick. I had told Elaine that I was going to take a break and stay on my own for a week to let everything settle down and give us a chance to reflect on our relationship and what we would be losing.

I spoke to Jenni before she went to bed trying to explain what was going to happen. She stood up, went up stairs, and never spoke to me again for three years. I was devastated and heart-broken as Jenni is my first born and we had a very special relationship.

Elaine came down from our bedroom and insisted I leave the house immediately. Jonathan appeared next, crying, having been woken up by our heated discussion.

Elaine held open the front door and demanded that I leave right now. Eventually I went to avoid any further upset for the children. I regret that I had not been stronger and stood up to her.

I found out later that she thought I was having an affair with a girl called Alison who ran the Victim Support network in Northumberland.

I had been on a training program to become a volunteer with the organisation. At the training sessions I had met a girl called Karen, who would two years later become my second wife.

From the moment I was kicked out of the family home there would be no return despite my attempts at reconciliation. I went back and talked to Elaine on three occasions but she had made up her mind that we would never get back together.

This is on reflection is the biggest regret of my life and in dark moments I wish I had had the courage just to end my life at that time, especially since my second wife walked out on me, in a very cruel manner.

The divorce turned out to be particularly unpleasant as Elaine turned into a very different character with a venomous vengeance of a woman scorned.

I lost all of my so called friends as they took the side of Elaine and spurned me for their own selfish reasons. You definitely find out who your real friends are during a divorce.

I went to live in Alnwick after the first couple of nights spent with Karen in her small flat. She was really kind to me and we formed a close friendship, which developed into a sexual affair while still married to Elaine.

I got a flat for myself which had mould and fungus growing in the bedroom. The shower fell apart every time I turned it on and there was one storage radiator which I could not afford to turn on. In the living room there was a coal fire but I had no money for fuel, so I acquired wood and coal from various sources without paying. Needs must prevail when the Devil calls.

I spent the most miserable Christmas for the first time in my life without family or friends and eventually I could not stand the pain of it all, feeling suicidal, so I called my Mum in Windsor asking for money to come and visit them.

So, poor me, but I was not alone, and the emptiness in my life helped me to form a strong spiritual bond with my Higher Power and for that I am grateful.

I remained on benefits for a year while I went to college part time and conducted my defence of the divorce proceedings with the help of a ball busting female solicitor.

At college I studied to be a counsellor and worked voluntarily for Victim Support. I found my health was deteriorating while living in the dampness of the cottage/flat in Alnwick. Thankfully I had the presence of mind to contact a housing agency who gave me an upstairs flat in one of the less desirable parts of the town but it was clean and dry and had a view over the castle, so that was an improvement.

I spent quite a lot of time around at Karen's flat although I always came back to my own to sleep. Then one day at Karen's request we went on holiday to the Greek Island of Aegina. I had never been so hot and uncomfortable in my life but I enjoyed the experience because I was with Karen, who would have been twenty four then and full of energy. I actually surprised myself as I matched her enthusiastic prowess in bed. We both got thrush and nappy rash, the latter from sitting on plastic seats in 40 degrees of heat. Quite an adventure considering my sheltered past, ha ha!!

While we holidayed, Jonno was asked to keep an eye on my flat and I gave him a key, big mistake.

He invited all his pals around to the flat for a party, all sixteen years of age and full of drink and drugs. They found my air gun and rifle in the cupboard, so in their inebriated state thought it a fabulous idea to shoot at all my pottery which I had made over the past year. After they bored themselves with the flat they proceeded to shoot the street lights out at which point a friend of his sister, Jenni, took the guns off him and sent them packing before the Police arrived.

When I returned from the holiday I have to say I was more than a wee bit aggrieved. I called Jonno, we met up and I took him to the Police Station and asked one of the officers whom I knew through the Victim Support to arrest him and give him a grilling to scare him, which duly worked very well and kept him from getting a record for possession of a fire arm.

The night before the court case to settle the finances, I received a phone call from Jonathan to inform me that his Mother had put the dog down. Ben, the dog had been my best friend for twelve years and the only reason he was not with me was because I wanted the children to keep him. It had been bad enough losing their Father and not knowing the real reasons why.

The divorce plodded on and eventually a hearing took place in the Crown Court building, Newcastle upon Tyne.

Anyone who may have been through this process will know how emotionally draining it is and also how dishonest and manipulative lawyers and ex wives are. It was all about the money now so in had to defend myself or end up with nothing but my shirt. I had worked hard all my life, despite the addiction problem and wanted to redeem some of the things I had been denied access to for the past year.

The opposition, my wife and her lawyers dragged up any dirt they could find but I stayed fair, reasonable, polite and honest throughout the three hours of questioning by her team.

I think in the end the Judge became fed up with their behaviour and told them to desist from their approach or he would take appropriate action, whatever that was we never found out as they gave up the onslaught. It is amazing what you can do if you keep to these principals.

God looked after me that day and I came out spiritually well with not much money to show for it but a clean spirit. I am surprised I managed after the incident with the dog which I believe was designed to derail me before the court case. Within a few months the divorce went through to decree absolute and that part of my life terminated.

LIFE AFTER DEATH
TWENTY SEVEN

The death of my first marriage and loss of contact with my children must surely be the most painful and emotionally devastating episode of my life up to that point. There is more to come, not through choice the next time but more of an example of how self centred people can be even when they do not suffer from an addictive personality.
I think the emptiness I felt inside due the loss of my loved ones from my life allowed me to experience spiritual growth. It helped me realise and accept some of my character assets. There were things I could do but also things I could not. I could find forgiveness and the ability to let go of emotional disturbance, I could not find it in my heart to seek retribution despite others targeting my sensitivities in the material and spiritual world.
Having my own space and responsibilities helped me to mature with nothing to fall back on expect my own decision making.
The relationship between Karen and I grew into true, deep feelings for her and for the first time I let go to embrace what I believe to be unconditional love. However I do not think Karen felt the same way.
When she was six years old she had to deal with the effects of a Father who suffered from a Gambling problem and later a Mother who displayed symptoms of a drink problem.

Then she goes and agrees to marry a recovering Alcoholic
who has just been through a divorce, been made redundant
part of his family will not even communicate with him. Oh,
and no professional standing in the world what so ever!!
It is really no wonder that her diabetic Mother lost the plot
when she heard of the prospects of her future Son-in-law.
She did come around I think more for the sake of her
daughter than a liking of me.
She displayed her disapproval and true feelings on several
occasions in the coming years which will become evident in a
later chapters and revelations.
It is possible Karen may have been damaged psychologically
by the desertion of her Father and the apparent Alcoholism
that her Mother displayed through Karen's early teenage
years.
Two years later and after the divorce, our relationship took
another dimension when I asked her to marry me. I
remember it well, we were in her flat on the couch chatting
wand listening to music.
After I popped the question she said ' I will tell you in five
minutes'. She left the room, went to the Loo, and returned to
give me an affirmative answer but with conditions.
We were to marry by the end of the month. When Karen
made a decision it was now or never which was one of the
things I admired about her.
I asked her on the 1st of October 1994 and we were married
on the 23rd October 1994. In this time the bands were read in
church, the cake ordered with three tiers, the top one for
diabetics with no sugar, the second with no Alcohol for the

Alcoholics and the final layer for the normal everyday tossers that enjoy booze in the recipe.

Karen's dress, boots and whip were all tailored as she dressed as a Rider and we had a reception for 120 people in a hotel beside a lake. There were 70 guests at the wedding itself, a Scottish Piper, two female Ushers and my Son, Jonathan was my best man.

The day was windy and murky but we had a very special time and everyone joined the festivities, dancing and socialising. Karen and I slept the night in the hotel. I was sick as I had consumed too much orange juice topped up with a cup of hot chocolate before bed, big mistake, but the marriage did get consummated on my recovery.

The honeymoon was spent in Amsterdam on a Boatel. We went around the sites visiting the diamond factory, Anne Frank's house and ate in a different restaurant each night. The classic choice was an Ethiopian place with four black African guys sitting at a table and a menu written in a foreign language. We were flying blind that night, but had a really good time mimicking cows, sheep and chickens to identify the meals on the menu card. Whatever it was that we ordered came on a very large plate in the centre of the table with large pancake things and no knife or fork. We must have sat there for ten minutes waiting for the utensils much to the amusement of the other guests. In Ethiopia they don't use cutlery as they pick up the food with the pancakes. Embarrassing but educational and I and sure it provided great entertainment for the staff.

I attended college in Newcastle University studying business and finance and had taken a few days off the course for the honeymoon so it was back to work after five days holiday.
I also went to Ashington College at the same time studying for a counselling diploma.
Being my first return to education since I was at school the learning curve was very steep but I managed both with flying colours.
We bought a house after the divorce finances were sorted in Choppington, beside one of the most notorious estates around for bad behaviour and criminality, which made for great entertainment on a Friday and Saturday night as the Police vans, cars and helicopter flew up and down the road. We stayed in that house for about six years, eventually moving to Widdrington Station and a three bed bungalow in a cul-de-sac overlooking the countryside.
In our last year at Francis Street, Choppington, Karen wanted to take up Shotokan Karate. I had already run my own club at Wooler so I thought I might take it up again, but this time I would be doing it sober. I donned my black belt and we went to the local club where I was definitely out of my depth as I had not practiced or trained for ten years or so. On the first night we did some fighting and I was paired with a six foot black belt second dan. Needless to say I ended up with a broken nose but managed to hold my own and not disgrace myself.
I worked hard at relearning my Katas and eventually became an instructor with the Karate Union of Great Britain. It was

very satisfying to prove to myself that I can do something sober which thought I could never do without a drink.

My Mother died in 1996 so she never met Alisha which is very sad as she would have loved her they are very alike physically and they are also very similar in personality, in fact sometimes I think Mum is reincarnated within Alisha. Mum's funeral must be one of the proudest moments of my sobriety in contrast to my Father's funeral where I behaved badly full of the poor me and vodka. I looked after my family and children as a proper Father should at their Grannies final goodbye.

Alisha was two years old when we moved to the bungalow and we had six great years enjoying the solitude of the small town. I decorated the whole house before we moved in and Alisha used to come with me. She used to put the screws from my tool kit in the locks, pretending they were keys. Some were easier to extricate than others but she had great fun laughing at my concern while I searched everywhere for the screws when I needed them, little tinker.

I used to take Alisha to pre-school nursery in the community centre beside the local school. I waited while watching her play together with her new friends. I sat at the side chatting to mothers of the other children. I formed a particularly close friendship with one of the Mothers. Her son and Alisha had become close friends along with another wee boy.

When the kids became of age to move on to primary school we all chose to send them to a country C of E school at Tritlington. It was the better option for our children as the local school catered for the whole community and some of them were less interested in education than our offspring. One particular Mother and I used to share lifts taking the children to school as it was five miles away. She also worked as a nurse in Wansbeck hospital and by this time I was a Paramedic, so we had a lot in common. We also liked each other a lot which she put down to the exchange of pheromones causing a sexual attraction. The only solution for these feelings was to keep away. To this day we still have the same attraction and so we still keep away from each other as she is now happily married again after her husband died. That was my last and final attraction to another woman, for which I am neither proud nor regretful , and Karen has also since left me in a very unfortunate way.

After the six years of happiness in the bungalow, where Alisha and I were very content, Alisha still talks about how she loved Widdrington and the house, but Karen became discontent again so a move was inevitable. That resulted in the move to the Canary Islands within a very short space of time in 2006. Karen became the Head Teacher at Hawthorne school in Ashington, which at her tender age of thirty two was a great achievement. She was well respected by her staff, pupils and parents and when she resigned to take up a post in the Canaries she was given a fantastic send off by the whole school and the Governors.

Unfortunately the incident leading up to her making a decision to leave involved a paedophile male teacher, the police and the county council. She had investigated certain events and complaints against the teacher and found them to be vilified. However she was not supported in her views by the county council as they wanted a cover up as usual to prevent any hassle or effort on their part. Consequently Karen fell out with them big style virtually taking every door off it's hinges on her exit from county hall, Morpeth. This was a very sad end to a very bright future for her career, but as Karen would say and did on many occasions 'Because I am like that, it's the way I am', no excuses needed just that show stopping statement which she used on many future crisis including her departure from the family home seven years later.

Well, it is probably time to move on to our adventure and experiences abroad now, but just before I do there is one more thing I need to write about and that is 'Fluffy ', the Great Dane.

Once again, if there were to be a decision made it had to come from Karen, not me!

I had wanted a dog all our married life but the idea was shelved each time as it was too tying and would make a mess of the house. That turned out to be a load of bollocks as Karen chose to have a Great Dane, another chance for her to shock and show off.

We bought the puppy from someone the cleaner knew, yes the cleaner! Now who's idea would that be I ask, to have a cleaner? Surprise, Karen needed a domestic 'pet' woman as well as a dog, but one that did the housework. I did the housework quite adequately before this intervention.

Fluffy was a beautiful boy and had a very soft nature. When Fluffy barked he scared himself and whoever wrote the cartoon character of Scooby Doo must have studied the character of a real Great Dane as Fluffy used to talk to us in an identical voice to Scooby Doo, a sort of grumbly surprised sound with a frown on his forehead, while his head would be cocked to the side in a questioning sort of pose.

He hated being on his own, Great Danes are very loyal and sociable so he showed his displeasure by eating his single bed mattress, the couch, the garden fencing and the whole of the back car seat once when I left him while I was away working on the ambulance. Despite all of that he was the most lovable dog I have ever had up to that point in my life.

One vivid memory happened when we were all out for a walk. Alisha would be five at the time and she loved Fluffy very much indeed, they used to roll about the floor together and she used to fall asleep on top of him. Anyway we were out for the walk and Fluffy began to slobber which dribbled into a long stream from his chops. Alisha took one look at it and puked on the pavement. Fluffy decided this was too good to resist and promptly ate it all up which in turn made Karen retch while I tried desperately hard to contain myself from rolling about the pavement laughing.

But all good things come to an end when married to Karen and I had to take Fluffy down to Lincolnshire, where he3 spent the rest of his days with eight other Danes on a farm. I remember his questioning facial expression for ever when I left him there. He looked so sad and I cried all the way home to Northumberland, regretting having left him. That is a lot of tears as it is 250 miles.

TWENTY EIGHT

We went on some cracking holidays before our daughter
Alisha was born in 1998.
I could bore the reader with six years of living together but I
won't do that to you. Instead I shall describe our holidays
together which were more than amazing experiences for a
previously 'stay at home in the UK' person like me.
The first booking we made involved a twelve hour flight to
Goa in India. The holiday was booked through a travel agent
to stay in a hotel that did not boast more than one star. We
went in April which would be just before the start of the rainy
Monsoon season so the heat we experienced was something
entirely new to me at around 30 degrees and on the last two
days 50 degrees and very humid so I poured with sweat for
two weeks as the hotel had no air conditioning, only a fan in
the middle of the ceiling which proved to be great
entertainment as we took turns to lie directly under it,
completely naked. So when it was Karen's turn I had two
good reasons for perspiring as she lay spread-eagled above
the sheets. There was indeed a lot of physical activity as a
result of this promiscuous behaviour. No complaints there on
my part.
Goa is an amazing place with two main religions, Christianity,
brought across by the plundering Portuguese and the native
Hindu of the Indians. I remember being told by someone who
had already visited Goa that it was advisable to have a look in
the front of the cab before you got in, if it had a cross
dangling from the mirror then it would be safe to travel. If it

had Hindu charms, then avoid it at all costs as the driver held
the belief that there is not much value in his own life, so there
would not be in yours either as they drove down the middle
of the road expecting everything to get out of their way. The
accident rate in India is staggering and often fatal.

The hotel was about three hundred yards from the beach.
The pathway that led to the sands trailed through a shanty
town of hut with palm roofs and a waste disposal pig in a pen
which doubled as the resident's toilet flusher. The native
Goans are lovely people who at our time of meeting them
were particularly unspoilt by contact with the outside world.
However they had not managed to avoid to poisons of our so
called advanced society, discovering alcohol but without any
cultural defence against its addictive properties.

They men were all fishermen with grand sized rowing boats
which they took out in all weathers and sea conditions. When
they returned to the shore they stack their boats on the
beach. Unloaded their catch and proceeded to consume
copious amounts of local beer, ending in unconsciousness on
the sand where they remained until early morning when they
re-embarked their vessels to catch more fish ad infinitum.

We travelled around Goa by taxi, Christian taxi. We tried to
visit a safari park which had various wild animals roaming
loose and had advertised the presence of Tigers, which I have
never seen in a natural habitat. We hailed a taxi from outside
the hotel explaining in English where we wanted to go and set
off for the adventure. When in a foreign country it is
advisable to have an interpreter to verify that the driver
knows what you have just told them. In this case we neither

had an interpreter nor much common sense so we ended up miles from anywhere at a deer park. The taxi left before we knew this was not the safari park so we were left stranded in the middle of somewhere in Goa. We asked if could get a taxi back but there were none then we asked how much would it cost us to stay the night in their accommodation. The charge would be fifty pence a night for the chalet so we decided to take a look as it would be exciting and another adventure, until that is, we saw the bathroom. It was a hole in the ground and a big green frog jumped out as we entered. The girls panicked and that was it, we would do anything to get out of this place ASAP.

At that moment a Tuc Tuc three wheeler cab pulled up but only had one seat. Karen gave the driver the equivalent of a pound to go and get us two taxis to take us back to the hotel. We had come with another family from the hotel with whom we had made friends. Nobody had any faith that we would see this guy again or any taxis either. After an hour of discussion we all agreed that we would stick it out and take the chalet, but just when we reluctantly came to this decision two taxis pulled up out of the blue to take us home. Oh ye of little faith said Karen.

The other place we visited was the Hippy Market at Anjuna Bay. It had been a tourist attraction since the Hippies is the early seventies had gone to Goa to escape the rigours of a capitalist world. A lot of them were bikers and the rest were spaced out junkies on Grass. This was my first attempt at bartering for trinkets and souvenirs. I have always been pretty lousy at bartering but it was brilliant fun as the sellers were mostly Indian from cities like Bombay and Calcutta. My one lingering memory of this experience was everybody rolling around the ground laughing as I was persitantly butted up the rear end by a cow with very large horns, which of course in India are sacred and you are not allowed to hit back, just get the hell out of there instead.

So that was our first adventurist holiday, totally brilliant but just a wee bit too hot.

The next place we chose was something I had only dreamt about never thinking it would come true, a real life safari in the Masi Mara, in Kenya.

We stayed in the Blue Marlin Hotel in Malindi, where the author Hemmingway wrote one of my favourite books, 'The old man and the sea'.

When we arrived at the hotel, Karen and me, decided to have a look around the local town. It was full of hussle and bussle like a wee market town should be. The streets were dusty earth and the buildings built of concrete blocks or of wood and mud.

The local people made a real fuss of us asking us to join in and have a go at making some of the wooden carvings and the teacher rushed out of the school hut inviting us to come and listen to the children singing. It really was a magical experience and one I will never forget. The happy smile on the kids faces, despite the fact or maybe because of the fact, they had virtually nothing but the clothes on their backs, just a great sense of spiritual well being.

That was a wonderful morning. We went back to the hotel full of the joys of life to have a coffee and attend the welcome meeting, which are normally really boring and a chance for the holiday reps to scare the holiday makers into believing they are in great danger unless we book with their organised tours.

The first instruction from the rep was a dire warning about leaving the hotel without first taking off all your jewellery and gold as two tourists had been attacked the previous week just around the corner on the beach. They were robbed of everything and that is why the guards are on the doors, to keep out the thieves.

Oops, naughty us, we still had our gold rings and chains on during our visit to the town. Maybe we were just lucky as when we returned home after the holiday the news reported that a coo had started in Kenya and tourists were advised not to go for the time being.

Part of our holiday was spent on the Masi Mara region where the wildlife and animals are protected from poachers. We decided to book our own tour as the holiday company wanted twice the price of the local firms.

Never the less it still cost us 700 pounds for two days safari, but it is the best 700 pounds I have ever spent.

TWENTY NINE
Safari in Kenya – Africa

This was an amazing trip with adventure written all over it. We stared off being driven to an air strip where we were to board our plane to take us over Mount Kilimanjaro on our way to the Massi Mara.

A private jet landed on the runway and pulled up in front of us. We thought we had landed on our feet this time as the plane was spanking new and seemed quite luxurious as we moved forward with our overnight bags to board. Only to be held back by the flight staff to allow some posh looking bloke and his bit of stuff to be allowed to enter first. Fair enough I thought, they look like they have paid for the posh seats so let them have their moment of superiority.

However when the door closed behind them leaving us on the tarmac, I gathered there may be some misunderstanding as the plane taxied to the runway and departed as quickly as it had appeared.

What now you might ask? We waited a further thirty minutes, all the time being told by the guy who had brought us to the airstrip 'Poli Poli' which means take your time and chill out in Swahili.

Next to arrive, drifting in at a much slower pace than the jet, was an 'Eagle Airways' turbo prop wreck of an aircraft which deafened us as we stood aghast at the sight of our transport. The door opened and a guy in a white shirt with official looking epilates placed an old rusty step on the ground and summoned us over. We boarded the plane to be greeted by a very enthusiastic pilot and placed in the old car seats that had been bolted to the floor. The air conditioning was a rubber fan placed near the cockpit. There were seventeen seats in all and eight of us travelling to our destination in the plains of Kenya to see the animals.

As the plane took off we could hear the stones hitting the bottom of the floor. The whole thing was so terrifying that I began to laugh and enjoy it with a sort of fatal acceptance that we were truly in the hands of God.

The flight took us about four hours flying very low, about 1000 feet above the ground. We hit turbulence from the heat rising off the baked earth and Karen, who is not the best of travellers began to fill the first sick bag thirty seconds after leaving Mother Earth.

I have never seen someone quite as relieved as Karen as we bounced down on the landing strip which was basically a track made with a JCB digger. Once again the stones battered the underside of the aircraft, but we were greeted by a very enthusiastic welcoming party who invited us to the airport shop. A mat on the ground covered in various beads and carvings which we duly bought as it would have been rude not to! That was the moment when Karen despaired as we were invited back on the plane. We were only dropping off half of the guests and were going on to a different destination. So we left the mud hut and mat on the ground. Bumping our way back into the air for a further half hour, to another similar runway. On landing the pilot came out of the cockpit seat and said what a marvellous job his assistant had done landing the plane as it was his first time ever flying this aircraft. Oh God help us, and I think he definitely did just that.

After disembarking we were led to a group of tents beside which was a large swimming pool. Our tent was massive and when we entered, accompanied by 'our boy' who would look after all our needs. We were greeted by at marble bathroom, two four poster beds and a plate of the freshest fruit I have ever tasted.

As we rested after the torturous flight, it was for Karen anyhow, there was a really loud roar from outside the tent. Karen nearly pooped herself and insisted I go out to investigate. Our 'boy' had left by now so man the hunter in my cowboy hat opened the flap to peek out. Nothing in sight, so a little bit further for a better view, still nothing. That's it I thought, go the whole hog, so I did. I got that feeling I had experienced in the plane of fete a compli, and just do it!! I ventured further outside to find a river about thirty feet below filled with the most dangerous beasts in the jungle, hippopotamuses.

They kill more tourists and local people than all the other animals put together. I, thankfully did not know this until the next day when being educated by our guide, Caesar.

We were introduced to Caesar the next morning at six o'clock after being tucked into bed the night by our 'boy' who brought us hot chocolate and a hot water bottle. Bazaar in the middle of Africa, as he came with our night time delights, I happened to be on the toilet having a poo. He was very polite, knocking before entering the tent. The toilet may have been made of marble but the door to it is not a door, in fact there was no door, so as Karen said 'come in' to our 'boy' he was met with the vision of a white man on the loo, with a very red face, but I got my own back on her the next day, ha ha.

It is freezing cold at night in the Massi Mara, hence the need for a bottle and chocolate. We put our coats on the next morning for our first safari run in the pitch black to see the lions eating their kill. We saw the hyenas and heard them crunch the bones of their victims after the lions had finished. Next were the prairie dogs and then the vulchers. There was a definite pecking order as each creature waited their turn to demolish the prey.

There is no way to describe the sounds, smells and feelings we felt that morning, just utter exhilaration.

We saw the 'big five' as they call them. We walked right next to the black rhinos, just feet away from them with only a young Masi boy with a stick to protect us. We flew over a herd of elephants, saw crocodiles in the rivers and chased down a leopard. We stopped in the jeep driven by Caesar, right beside a pride of lions basking in the heat of the day and that was when Karen got her comeuppance for her dirty trick with the 'boy' the night before.

As we parked by the lioness and her cubs, the mother took exception to the intrusion and bounced forward with a mighty roar. I got a fantastic photograph and turned to Karen to tell her. She had disappeared, I looked down to find her on the floor of the jeep, cowering in terror. Job done, well done that lioness, I would never let her forget that in future accounts of our trips abroad to other people.

Buffalo, Ostriches and the famous Secretary bird all graced us with their presence over our four safari runs. They are definitely the most precious moments of my life so far and I hope my children and grandchildren get the same opportunity before the creatures are cast into oblivion by the selfish needs of the human beings.

The trip back from there was no less eventful as we flew through a storm and were diverted to Nairobi where we changed planes to a real one with stewardesses and a proper pilot. Returning to

the grounds of the hotel which were akin to a tropical paradise with two swimming pools and very luxurious rooms.

THIRTY
THAILAND

In 1997 we embarked on our final monster holiday, this time to Thailand. Four days in Bangkok followed by a complete rest on the Paradise island of Phuket at a resort called Karon Beach.

When arriving after a ten hour flight mid-morning it is advisable to try and stay awake until bedtime but when Karen and I saw the five star bed in the four star hotel in the middle of Bangkok it took only a few minutes to fall asleep. I don't think we arose until the next morning to a hearty breakfast and then on to explore the smog of the Capital City. Traffic in Bangkok sits nose to tail almost all day and night so we copied the locals and held a handkerchief over our mouths. When we took them away it left a big black mark where the breath and smog filtered through. I do not know how people would want, or choose to live in such a place. Children adorned every corner, begging from us tourists. Most of them had a disability to foster our sympathies, many of them broken arms or legs inflicted by their parents deliberately, to make them into these creatures of tragic deprivation.

In contrast to these images were the golden palaces created for the royal family in celebration of their Buddhist beliefs. We visited the temples, respectfully removing our shoes in order to enter the places of worship.

To our delight they held the world championship Thai Boxing competition while we were there and we managed to procure a couple of ringside tickets from our hotel.

As we entered the large circular hall everybody suddenly stopped and stood very still. We did the same more through fright than respect, thankfully we did as they were playing the nation anthem.

Would have been awful to get thrown out before we got in! The noise inside the stadium was truly deafening until the fighters appeared to perform their respectful tributes to Buddha. Then the excitement increased as the audience started to bet on the outcome of each fight, always before the fighters entered the ring. Then the rhythmic clanging of bells and beating of drums raised the atmosphere to an almost catatonic level.

It was a really fantastic experience and we were two of only eight foreign visitors to be present which made us feel very special. We were quite exhausted after the three hours of mayhem.

We haled a taxi back to the hotel, through the nose to tail traffic. It would have been quicker walking if knew where the hotel was so we had to put up with sitting in the taxi for 30 minutes. The driver was taking a sip out of a bottle filled with a milky liquid which the hotel porter informed us was Methadone. That must have been the reason we had to keep waking up the driver to move forward in the queue of traffic. Thank God we never went over ten miles an hour all the way back.

In the morning we hunted out a tailor's shop to be measured up for suits, jackets and dresses and trousers in Cashmere material and I still have and wear the suit today, which will be twenty years old now.

While in Bangkok I decided to go to an Alcoholics Anonymous meeting. Karen went to the hairdressers in the hotel to get pampered while I was out and about.

I went to the taxi rank armed with a card I had been given by a friend in the fellowship who often visited Thailand for business purposes. I showed the card to the first driver who shook his head in a negative manner passing me onto the next in line. None of them seemed to know where this place was, either that or they did not want to go to the place indicated on the card.

I was about to return to the hotel lobby when a Thai guy in a suit took the card from me and said something to the first driver and I was bundled into the back of the taxi which took off with me as a kidnap hostage. At least that's what went through my mind but I was powerless to protest.

After a few miles I began to think I might be right until he pulled up outside a large back street building and pointed to a door in the distance. He took the fare and drove off leaving me somewhere in Bangkok. I knocked on the door only to be shocked by a guy who came up behind me and ushered me in through the entrance saying 'are you a friend of Bob and Bill', my heart jumped in delight as I realised I had entered the meeting room which was evidently in the rear of the American Embassy.

I was so relieved and began to feel safe once more. There were twenty recovering Alcoholics there from all over the world. A fantastic meeting run under the same guidelines as all other meetings in the world. When I related my journey to the meeting they all laughed about the taxi and said it was not surprising as most of the drivers cannot read or write. With that cosy feeling of comfort one can only get at a meeting of AA I left saying goodbye to all my newly made friends in the fellowship. That feeling very quickly dissipated with the realisation that I had no idea where I was in a city of nine million inhabitants. I walked along the streets trying to find a major highway to catch a taxi but there were none to be seen. Just then a three wheeled Tuc Tuc came around the corner which I flagged down and asked for the Majestic hotel and we were off.

I did get back to the hotel safely with a feeling of complete relief and a sense of wellbeing that I had managed to get a meeting in a strange city where I had no idea of the language. God looked after me that night and also thanks to that mystery gent who put me in the taxi at the hotel.

The next day we set off for Phuket by plane. The country and seas around Phuket are very beautiful and so different from the coast of the UK. The waters are warmer for a start although we never swam in the sea as we had a magnificent pool at our new five star hotel in Karon Beach resort. There were not many guests as it was just going out of season so that made it all the more enjoyable having the place to ourselves apart from a few couples from the UK.

We visited the islands of Ko Samui where James Bond movies were filmed and ate in some tremendous restaurants out at sea and on the land. The couple next door to our room were on their honeymoon and seemed to like our company so we went out to the local town for nights out together.

The bars there featured Lady Men as entertainment. Men who had had a sex change to female

They were actually very attractive to look at and I could imagine that some male tourists on their own might make a few errors of judgement when choosing a date for the night, or maybe that is why some of the guys went there, to fulfil their sexual desires.

Thailand has to be the most relaxing holiday I ever had even though Karen had one of major monthly strops while we were there.

The holidays continued on a regular basis but a wee bit more modest in their adventure to Spain, Majorca, France, Austria and Switzerland, in fact all over Europe.

I think Alisha must be one the most travelled children I know. She is very culturally aware as a result and should have set her up for life as a non judgemental individual just like her sister and brother, Jenni and Jonno.

COVERING 3 OF YEARS NHS SERVICE - DOCTOR DEATH – THE GRIM REAPER – AKA, ARTHUR BIGGS

PLACE	AGE	GENDER	INCIDENT
A1 Alnwick	25	Male	Hit by car at 70 mph lost leg and fingers - deceased
Sharperton	21	Male	Driver – hit tree at 70mph - head and internal – died last breath on road - witnessed
Blyth	30	Male	Beaten – baseball bat – combatant and threatened to kill me - died after 12 hours
Blyth	47	Male	Beaten with table leg – face fell apart on touching for examination – died 12 hours – person who did it in room with us – his son
Alnwick	6	Male child	Foot off after accident in car park – had to stick foot back on.
Bedlington	80	Male	Daughter had to be pulled off father with rigor mortis – had been dead up to 12 hours
Durham	90	Female	Naked in shower – suspicious death – police called
Alnwick	27	Male	Had to cut down – hanging from banisters – got back

			then lost vital signs again - dead
Warkworth	48	Male	Immediately after hanging called to find man dead in caravan in own pool of vomit.
Amble	19	Male	Wrapped up in car around tree – dead – hit tree at 100 mph
Amble	15	Male	Thrown thro woods at height of 8ft died later in hospital – internal bleed hit tree at 100mph
Amble	15	Male	Thrown thro woods at 100 mph – bits of brain sticking out still screaming after one hour – died in hospital next day
Berwick	50	Female	Died in car park could have been saved but meal break more important for other crew – management fault
Amble	22	Male	Stabbed in Greek take away - survived
Seaton Del	60	Male	On floor for several days – black and smelly
Blyth	60	Female	On floor for three days still alive but messy
Morpeth	70	Male	Still in bed dead for several

			days - stinky
Cramlington	30	Female	30 stone – cardiac arr. – mouth and lungs full of vomit could not move her despite efforts
Alnwick	35	Female	Dead on arrival had to wait 2 hours with body in one room apartment for police to arrive
Widdrington	70	Male	CPR but lost patient
Holywell	60	Male	Cardiac arrest in front of whole family shouting - lost patient horrible experience
Berwick	25	Female	Head on – lady dead but transgressor still alive – still have to go to court to give evidence
Morpeth	25	Male	Asthma – restart resps in front of doctors – Mr. Hume was my partner that day good job
Stannington	47	Male	Massive CVA – kept alive but died in A & E
Mitford	35	Female	Suicide – respiratory failure but survived.
Bedlington	16	Male	Meningitis – mother spirit healer so did not call till too late – died next day

Berwick	48	Male	Card arr. in bus shelter – took to mortuary
Berwick	60	Male	Card arr. In bed tried CPR no good – wife had card arr. downstairs - survived
Berwick	80	Male	Father of paramedic – card Arrest – DOA (dead on arrival) – whole family present – M and C (Monitored and confirmed)
Ashington	75	Female	Dead in chair in nursing home (NH) M and C
Ashington	80	Female	Dead in bed in NH – (M and C)
Ashington	70	Female	Dead in chair in NH – M and C
Berwick	80	Female	DOA – NH - M and C
Bedlington	65	Male	DOA – M and C
Alnwick	19	Female	BABY DELIVERED IN HOUSE – BREACH BIRTH – MOTHER AND CHILD DOING WELL – SURVIVAL DUE ENTIRELY TO MY MATE COOGIE AND ME – THANK GOD FOR THAT!!!!!!!!!!!!!!!!!!!!!!!!!!!!!!!!

THIRTY TWO

One might expect there to be many traumatic incidents in the life of a Paramedic. However some are more fortunate than others. The above list depicts my own experiences.

At first when I started out on the road I longed for the excitement and adrenaline rush produced by the emergency buzzer and the rush to be on the road with the blues and twos shining and blaring to warn the public of the approaching angels of mercy in our chariot of salvation.

This vocation attracts personalities like mine. A deep altruistic desire to help and make a difference in life and death situations, but also, an initial feeling of self importance and a childish super hero disposition born from a previous existence of little self worth. At least that is how it was for me.

The following various incidents describe how I gradually developed Post Traumatic Stress Disorder (PTSD). I try my best to describe the feelings and atmosphere around each incident but I cannot purvey the smell, sounds, and the hot, cold or wet conditions I experienced in the raw atmosphere of the unnatural world of traumatic witness to situations, which were essentially beyond my control. Nor some of the threatening situations where potential patients were in a combative condition due to head injuries or intoxication.

My natural magnetic attraction for extreme trauma is one of rarity and I expect many Ambulance personnel will be grateful for that.

On one hand I regret the PTSD and a broken marriage which I believe were the consequences of my reputation as a

'Trauma Magnetic' and the nick names of 'Doctor Death' and 'The Grim Reaper'. The name calling I wore as a medal to begin with but that wears very thin when colleagues response to my shift pattern was one of avoidance, 'Oh no not you again that means a bad shift'.

So here goes I will try to convey what it was like, how I felt and how initial enthusiasm and excitement turned to fear and dread of another shift.

THIRTY THREE
INCIDENTS

My last three years with the Ambulance Service were very traumatic and quite unusual although not unheard of due to the nature of the job.

Some people are just unfortunate I suppose and I believe that I was one of them. In fact if you asked the majority of my colleagues they would most likely agree.

Hence the handle of 'Doctor Death' and the 'Grimm Reaper' imposed upon me by my partners at various stations across Northumberland.

At first I appreciated the comical side of the nicknames. But after a while, when I started to believe they may be right and that I was indeed a 'Trauma Magnet' I began to experience anxiety before each shift. What was coming next?

I will résumé the incidents, some with great detail and others grouped into specific categories, in an effort to understand my normal reactions to abnormal situations. Hopefully this will help me to understand the onset of my Post Traumatic Stress Disorder (PTSD).

I was not long out of Paramedic school having passed my final exams despite the aggressive and vindictive behaviour of all but one of the instructors, he was a jovial and very knowledgeable instructor called Jim. My eternal thanks go to him for giving me self-worth and belief in myself to endure the rigorous attentions of the other members of staff. I was not alone in my opinion as every student eventually

complained about the treatment and the staff were
eventually disciplined or indeed retired.

Passing the exams and qualifying from the college after three
months of being away from my family only covered the
academic and practical learning with pencils and plastic dolls,
now we would experience first-hand responsibility for
people's lives in the raw world of reality.

The next 12 months were spent with mentors on the road
who had many years of experience. I began to love the job
and always looked forward to my next shift.

How can I describe the first shift as a qualified Advance
Technician on the Ambulance? It really is quite a daunting
experience, very exhilarating with emotions running from
fear to a feeling of self-worth which I do not believe any other
profession can give an individual.

When that first emergency buzzer went off in the station, I
almost hit the ceiling as my mentor looked on and said 'this
too shall pass'.

On the way to the emergency he gave me some very sound
advice which I have never forgotten and has stood me in
good stead since that day.

He advised that I should remember that all the people we
treat are vulnerable. However, the most acute emotions are
very often from the on-lookers who may be family, friends or
even the general public as we are dealing with abnormal
circumstances on most occasions.

The second piece of advice is also engrained on my psyche.
Never rely totally on the machines we are trained to use, but
more to rely on our senses of sight, touch, hearing, smell and

speech. Ask as many questions as possible even if I think they are fundamental or it is obvious that I think I already know the answer.

I of course ignored all of this advice as the adrenalin rushed through my body on approaching the first very seriously ill patient of my career.

We entered the bedroom where the gentleman was sitting up in bed and his daughter appeared to be giving him a hug. I gathered my thoughts and remembered the protocol of questions to ask. But my Mentor rushed in and pulled the daughter aside giving me a clear view of the guy in the bed. He did not look well at all in fact he looked like a marble statue, he was quite a greyish yellow colour. Remember to use my senses, but that is not always easy when under stress. What happened next was so unexpected it appeared comical. My Mentor grabbed the guy's legs and pulled him hard towards the bottom of the bed. The gentleman in question, the patient, came down the bed still sitting upright. He was dead and had been for many hours as the rigor mortis set in making his body rigid.

So that was my first encounter with a dead body which has given endless hours of amusement to all the other Paramedics and fuel for jokes for years to come.

You can make up your own jokes if you like, the possibilities are endless.

As a Paramedic we were allowed to diagnose death by means of physical examination, fix and dilated pupils, no pulse, no breathing or pooling of blood at the lowest point of the body. The forms had to be particularly meticulous due to the seriousness of the responsibility as we could be called to give evidence in a court of law as to the patient's demise.

So that was my first dead body and certainly not my last. There was a certain humour to this incident but little did I know they are not all as simple and definitely more bloody and gory.

On reflection I was a good paramedic and respected by most of my colleagues and managers with few exceptions.

I also had many thanks conveyed by the patients by word of mouth and also testament. I am proud of this and do not regret any of the ambulance work.

Thirty four

I was called to eight further emergencies involving elderly ladies and gentlemen who had passed away peacefully or at least I hope they went without pain or trauma, but who knows? However not all of these lay quietly in bed. Four had died in nursing homes while sitting sleeping overnight in their chairs and were found the next morning by staff who called 999 for an ambulance. One gentleman we found lying on the kitchen floor and had been there for more than a week, needless to say the body was particularly smelly and very black in colour.

We got a call from a neighbour of the next patient to say they were worried as they had not seen the old lady next door for three days but the house was all locked up and they were sure she was still inside. The police came and broke down the door for us to enter the premises where we found her in the back room. The odour in the house instigated involuntary retching in us both so we put the Vick under our noses in order to treat the patient who was covered in her own excrement, vomit and urine. She had fallen three days before our intrusion and broken her neck of femur bone so was unable to move to call for help.

Human resolve is quite amazing as she joked with us and unbelievably laughed about her being so stupid as to fall over her cat which had also added to the aroma in the house. Unfortunately she never fully recovered from her misadventure and died a week later. We did not always find out about the result of our care but we did enquire about this old lady as she had made a lasting impression with her resolve and courage.

The front line ambulance emergency service gave us very little time to rest on the twelve hour shift pattern and so there was no time to process some of the abnormal situations in which we were involved. It is concluded in research by universities across Europe and the USA that the PTSD condition is present in 25% of all front line ambulance staff. I hear of many claimants for trivial conditions, such as sore fingers from typing too much or some idiot tripping over a curb stone because they don't look where they are going. There are thousands of pounds awarded to these people. There are countless paramedics out there who could no longer work due to developing PTSD as a result of the selfless work they have done for humanity, but they are a forgotten statistic.

I cry for them as I am one myself. I sacrificed my safety and sanity and still I do not regret it but would love to see some recognition for the service they have provided.

Ok, so let's get back to the nitty-gritty of the seedier side of life.

Violence seems to be very prevalent in our society today, a part of life, which to be honest, I can do without, but we see it more and more on the media, in films and most repulsively in video games designed for children and condoned by many adults because it is not reality.

The reality is that it is all about the money, money, money! The global economy today thrives on the sale of arms, conflict and starvation. I wonder what humans have become?

Four of the seedier jobs involved murder or attempted murder of an individual.

The first was domestic violence within a council house. We arrived to find the police already on scene. The victim was a thirty five year old woman who had been hit over the head repeatedly with a hammer by her partner who had returned home drunk to a disgruntled female companion.

The next incident with this particular theme was the last job of the day on a shift down in Sunderland while I was on cover duty. It happened in a pensioner's bungalow and when we arrived some neighbours were fussing around the front door as both the police and ourselves drew up in our respective vehicles with the blues and twos shining in the dusky winter night's air.

The door of the bungalow had been clearly forced leaving a broken lock and shredded door support. As is usually the case the police went in first to assess the situation and we followed on the all clear from the officers. We found ninety year old lady completely naked in the shower room, propped up against the wall but the shower itself was turned off. I have never seen a sight quite like it. Her skin appeared all gnarled and was a dark brown colour, she looked like a dried prune hanging on a hook. There were no signs of life and we pronounced her dead on arrival (DOA) and the police logged it as a suspicious death. I never found out if there had been anything untoward about her death but the image still remains in my head today as one of the abnormal instances of my ambulance career, and plagued my dreams from time to time. Maybe if I had had closure by finding out the circumstances the incident I might have been able to clear it from my memory, who knows.

hirty Five

Number three was an emergency call to a telephone box in the middle of Blyth Port in Northumberland. The details were sketchy but the gist of the call suggested an unconscious and bleeding male in the phone box. When we arrived nobody appeared to be in the vicinity. The time was midday which is an unusual time for a call like this as they usually happen usually in the dark. We reached the phone box six minutes after the initial call was made to the emergency 999 line. This in the eyes of statistics is a success. We always used to say that if you get there in over eight minutes and save a life it goes down as a failure, making a mockery of the system and an insult to the intelligence of the crew. Who in their right minds would take their time to respond to an emergency call, it makes no sense!!

Anyhow, the victim of the assault was nowhere to be seen, the area seemed deserted. Until that is, a guy came round the corner covered in blood coming from a wound on his head.

I approached him and asked if he would like me to take a look at his injury but he pushed me away and I stumbled over a wee wall taking little comfort in the texture of the pavement as I landed.

I got back up and my partner tried to calm him down but he was having none of the caring and sharing approach.

He walked, or actually staggered off, in the direction of a house nearby, which he entered with familiar ease so we reckoned that may be where he resided.

We followed and knocked on the door to be greeted by a very attractive young lady. I only noticed that because we were trained to pay attention to all of the details!!

We told her what had transpired and she informed us that it was her husband and someone had hit him over the head with a baseball. He had gone off after the assailant and this was the first she had seen of him for thirty minutes after the assault.

We tried again in vain to persuade the guy to let us take a close look at the injury but he just put his head under the tap and told us to 'go forth and multiply' (a quote from Leviticus in the bible). But he shortened it to a well known phrase or saying involving two words, the first of which is not in the bible.

Another thirty minutes went by but he did not change his mind, he was not going to hospital. The wife became quite upset but there is nothing we could do if the patient chooses to refuse treatment. We left with some concern in our minds but told the wife to call again if the situation deteriorated.

We went back to the ambulance and reported the situation only to be told to leave as there was another emergency to cover. Both my partner and I were loathed to leave but we were powerless to intervene.

Later in the day we heard that a female crew had been called back to the same address by the police as the victim had started to smash the house up with the wife locked inside. She must have been terrified as we knew she had begged him to go to hospital when we had attended.

The police had to travel in the back of the ambulance with the patient and also handcuff him to the stretcher after the paramedic had administered a mild sedative.

On arrival at hospital it took seven male nurses and doctors to restrain him.

He did not survive the night as he died from a severe bleed in the brain which put pressure on the Medulla causing him to stop breathing which in turn stopped his heart, they call this 'coning'.

Thirty Seven

The final incident which ended with the patient dying in hospital happened in the same town and once again was an early call for such an incident.

We responded to a 999 call at 6pm on a Thursday night which again is not the normal time for an assault.

Again I was the active paramedic on the crew while my partner drove us to the address in Blyth. On arrival a woman greeted us at the door and I followed her into the property with the first response bag on my shoulder.

The place stank of vomit, the carpets were filthy and all sorts of rubbish lay around the floor, which is something to identify in case we needed a stretcher for the patient.

She ushered me into the living room which is a misnomer in this case as dying room would be more appropriate.

The patient sat slumped on the sofa, bleeding and salivating from the mouth. I wore my gloves as always and unwillingly placed my bag on the floor.

The man was in his late forties, sprawled over the couch like a rag doll. He responded to my questioning and approach with nothing but moans and groans, so I asked the woman and the young man sitting in the arm chair across the room what had happened.

The guy in the chair picked up his can of beer with one hand while smoking a cigarette with the other and replied that he had been responsible for the condition of the patient. He had smashed his father with the leg of the table repeatedly until he stopped hitting his mother. He concluded with a desire for his father to be dead.

This of course is not the language used by the family and most of it was less than cool and collected.

Thankfully at this moment the police had arrived as I felt less than comfortable with the situation of being trapped in a room with a dying man, the perpetrator and the beaten wife. At the time they came into the room I was examining the patient, I realised he had lost a lot of blood so I tried to attach the oxygen face mask, on doing so his face seemed to fall sideways which prevented the apparatus from fitting properly. A further investigation revealed serious facial injuries.

My partner went to the ambulance for the chair as we had assessed the stretcher would not pass by all of the debris in the hall and living room.

The Police officers arrested and cuffed the assailant leading him out to the awaiting squad car.

We followed them out with the patient and took him to hospital with an urgency I had not experienced before as the patient, a police officer and I held on for dear life in the back of the ambulance.

In these circumstances the driver contacted the hospital to alert them of our estimated arrival time and to have a team waiting in the resuscitation area.

Further investigation after the event revealed that the Father was an Alcoholic, who had returned home, beaten up the Mother and the Son had lost control of his anger, ripping the table leg off and beating his Father repeatedly. The injuries had suggested the Father was hit over fifty times with the weapon leaving multiple breakages both internally and externally.

The Father being an Alcoholic had a seriously damaged liver which could not produce the Fibrinogen needed by the body to induce the blood clotting process. So the Father died later that evening in hospital.

The Mother had called the ambulance on the night in question and the Son was locked up for the night to appear in court the next day where he was remanded in custody for the murder of his Father. The sad part of this tragedy is the Son hung himself in his cell shortly after being locked up, leaving the Mother alone.

Calls to disturbances were not unusual at the weekends but it is not the patient who creates the threatening atmosphere, it is the surrounding drunken behaviour and the fact that nearly everyone seems to become a qualified specialist in the patient's injuries after consuming copious amounts of drugs and alcohol.

On analysing my reactions to various incidents I find that I became de-sensitised to the violence and threatening behaviour. However it does make me react to situations with hyper vigilance and still today I cannot sit with my back to a door or empty space. I cannot walk down the road without checking to see what is behind me and if someone is following me down a street I will stop and let them pass.

Thirty Nine

There are many more violent incidents and I shall skim over a few without particular detail and here are two of them.

A taxi driver had been hit over the head with a pool cue in an argument in a bar. He was still walking about but on examination there was some of his brain starting to poke out of the injury. I have no idea if he survived but I think it is less than likely.

Out on the streets a young man woke up from unconsciousness and threatened to stab me if I did not back off. Later in the A & E dept. he repeated the threat but this time my partner and I put him in a cubicle and behind closed doors, out of earshot of the staff, we told him his lifespan would be acutely shortened if he opened his mouth again. He tried to make a complaint but it fell on deaf ears as the nurses were definitely not on his side.

Before I recount the vehicle accidents that finally tipped me over the edge there is one particular job that still remains in my memories as a tragedy that should never have happened and transpired as a direct result of financial decisions made by the CEO of the NEAS during the time I worked for them. I always thought and still have the same opinion today that the CEO should have been held culpable for corporate manslaughter through his arrogant and selfish desire to manipulate figures in order to meet his bonus targets.

There had been a meal break dispute between management and front line staff. We were on call during our breaks to answer emergency calls, which of course is just how it should be. But the new CEO decided that we would no longer be paid for these breaks as most of the time we were not called out, which was not true but they manipulated the figures to suit their unproven statistics.

The staff were now told they were no longer on call during these breaks. Even if a baby was dying round the corner the control room would not call us out but get an ambulance from further away to respond. This was tantamount to emotional blackmail as we are caring individuals who would never let anyone suffer as a result of a dispute. But what you don't know about you cannot respond to!

So a call came in to our station to attend a woman having a heart attack seventeen miles away. We put on the blues and twos but there was never any hope of reaching the lady in the time frame of eight minutes required for attending a cardiac arrest.

When we arrived 15 minutes later, which was good going, we found an unconscious female of about 50 years of age lying in the car park of a holiday caravan park. The husband had tried to do CPR (cardio pulmonary resuscitation) under the instruction of the control centre and we took over immediately we arrived. The monitor was attached to her ASAP but we found no heartbeat or   ventricular fibrillation so shocking her was not an option, however we continued with the CPR while calling for backup from the station one mile away from the incident. The two paramedics were on their meal break at the time of the emergency and were finally contacted and asked to attend. Unfortunately too much time had elapsed between the time of her collapsing and the time of our arrival so she was pronounced dead at the scene.

I felt helpless, powerless and very angry, that the lady may have had a fighting chance of survival had it not been for the pathetic meal break squabble caused directly by the obstinacy of an uncaring CEO of the NEAS.

To add to the trauma the lady's 12 year old daughter clung to me crying while we transferred her mother into the ambulance to take her to the mortuary.

As I said before, that wee girls cries and tears will haunt me forever.

Forty

Road traffic collisions were a frequent addition to our daily excitement, involving mostly cars, motorbikes or both.
One memorable biker accident happened in the middle of the A1 in Northumberland. He had come off his Harley Davison while on an outing with his Chapter as they called themselves. His leg was badly injured and needed further roadside examination. The leg had been under the bike as he skidded along the tarmac so he must have been in a fair amount of pain. However the body's protection system must have kicked in and the only thing he was concerned about was his leathers.
I informed him I would have to cut them off in order to assess the necessary treatment and equipment for his transportation to hospital but he was adamant I was not touching his leggings. It took a full twenty minutes and a fair amount of morphine to persuade him that things would only get worse for him if we delayed any further.
In the mean time the queues of traffic and onlookers (rubberneckers) had grown into an audience. It wasn't until I cut the leathers off that I realised he was not protecting his leathers but his dignity as he wore nothing at all under the garments.
So now we had a half naked Hells Angel and his pals all around who were not the most sensitive individuals when it came to taking the piss out of their incapacitated member (pun intended), excuse the pun!!!!

Some flash backs are more pleasant than others and the one I describe now is one of the worst episodes of my career. It made me very angry to the extent I found it difficult to keep a professional attitude. Paramedics are trained to be non-judgemental and only deal with the job in hand having no opinion on outside matters but at the end of the day we are human.

The collision occurred on the A1 north of Berwick on Tweed on a single carriageway with crash barriers to prevent any vehicle from falling over the 300 foot cliff and down to the sea and rocks beneath.

A young woman, 27 years of age was driving home on Christmas Eve, returning to her parents for the festive season. She drove on the south bound side of the road next to the crash barrier. Her speed according to the police must have been about 50 mph. This part of the road had a long sweeping bend to the right so she must have seen the wagon travelling at 40 mph. but there is no way she could have seen the car overtaking the wagon at seventy mph coming straight for her.

She had nowhere to go between the crash barrier and the wagon and collided with the maniac in the car.

There were two ambulances attending, one from Scotland and ourselves from Northumberland, four police cars and a fire engine.

The Scottish crew attended the young woman with our assistance but there was nothing any of us could do as her car had its roof ripped off along with the poor woman's head. It was then our job to attend to the other car driver who was still alive and trapped in his car which was now on its roof on the grass slope opposite the decapitated female.

The fire brigade propped up his car to avoid it rolling on top of me as I crawled under to climb in the window to assist my partner who was entering the vehicle by the passenger window as the car was at a 45 degree angle.

Neither of us wanted to be risking our lives for someone who smelt of alcohol and admitted to taking drugs when questioned before we gave him any pain relief.

But that is not how it works on a dark, windy and rain soaked night or any other night. Just do the job and have no opinions or feelings, impossible, but we managed the situation and saved the man's life.

Forty One

SHARPERTON to AMBLE
CHAPTER

Breeeep! I am standing on my feet, why? Because, when that buzzer goes off the adrenaline pumps through the body like an F1 Ferrari at the starting grid. A moment ago I was relaxing watching a program on TV, well, not really watching or relaxing, but resting in anticipation of another call. The TV is on while Steve, my paramedic partner for this 12 hour night shift, makes another cuppa for us both. My third cup since coming on duty at 6.30pm this evening. It is eleven thirty in the evening.

Already we have been out to a couple of 999 calls but nothing serious. Certainly not requiring our complete skills as one of the front line Emergency Ambulance Crews this evening. We cover the baron expanse of the North East of England. The calls were not hoax calls but ones that would have better required a home visit from a GP (General Practitioner). However in this day and age of progression the system provides one GP to cover an area of 2000 square miles with several pockets of dense population. Even for an accountant surely that cannot make sense, and it is accountants that govern the NHS nowadays. Hence the reason in these advanced days of technology and careful budgeting, there are not enough Ambulance Crews to cover this vast geographical area, nor GP's either it seems. The government in their wisdom decided to let the GP's opt out of working after six pm and at weekends. What would I do?

I have been working for the Ambulance Service since September 2000 and progressed to fulfil the duties of an Advance Technician. They call me 'Doctor Death' and on occasion the 'Grim Reaper'. I have been unfortunate enough to earn the titles. Thirty five of the 999 calls I have attended in the past three years have resulted in fatality, or were DOA, dead on arrival. I hasten to add that this is not a reflexion of my skills or those of my fellow crew members, just unlucky. I therefore received the titles afore mentioned and as I appear through the door of the Station for my duty I am being met with a groan from all a sundry that it is going to be 'one of those nights'. Funny to begin with, and quite flattering in an odd sort of way, but these jobs and titles can get under your skin without you noticing, and, without the appropriate support they can be quite dangerous for the psychological wellbeing of the 'Front Line Staff'. At the time of the Sharperton/Amble incidents appropriate care was not in place for any of the Ambulance Staff in the North East of England, and still isn't at the time of writing.

The buzzer alarm alerts us to a call, Steve is already on his way to the Ambulance which is parked in the garage nearby. We have 45 seconds from the buzzer going off to punch in mobile on the Ambulance. I am the Attendant tonight and Steve is the Driver for this shift. The Vehicle is already coasting out of the Garage as I lock up the Station and make my way to join Steve. I put on my seat belt and we are under way. I look at the Terrafix, a computerised system to ascertain the type and category of job we are about to attend.

It is a category A call, the most serious of the categories, which means it is immediately life threatening. To be honest these are the calls that we live and work for, even if they do wear us thin emotionally. We are life savers at heart and definitely adrenaline junkies. These alerts demand a speedy journey to the incident with our own safely in mind of course. This is bollocks as we seldom have concern for our own safety. Blue flashers lighting up the night sky and sirens blaring we make our way to Sharperton. Whether we admit it or not it gives us a feeling of importance in the great scheme of unimportant existence.

The anticipation is electric as I read out the description to my partner. An RTA, road traffic accident, has happened in a remote part of Northumberland. Why is the atmosphere tense? Because an RTA is not normally an 'A' response even if it is serious, and, Sharperton is Fifty miles from Amble. Did I mention before that we are short of operational vehicles and cover for the area? The reason for this anomaly of shortage of cover lies fairly and squarely in the hands of our illustrious leaders. They are accountants, not dedicated vocational people like the front line staff on the road. The Chief Executive decided not to pay the staff while eating our dinner, but still expected us to respond if a 999 call came in to the service. To save money not lives, perhaps!

Thirty minutes of terrifying travelling time at up to ninety miles per hour on country roads. It is midnight and there must have been a shower of rain earlier as the roads are damp and slippery. If you are the attendant you are in the hands of the driver until you reach the incident. Steve is a good driver thankfully but in the country you never know what is around any corner. There has already been one accident that we know of and we are on our way to find it's location. We have satellite navigation which can be accurate to twenty yards on some occasions but in the hills of Northumberland we can experience problems.

To our surprise we are contacted on the radio by control who start to direct us verbally. Most unusual but very helpful as it turns out, we are lost on the satellite navigation. We are guided into the exact spot to find several police vehicles have arrived seconds before us and have started to secure the area. There is a car in the middle of the road. Twisted and broken by an impact. It looks like the driver may have skidded on the bend and hit a tree.

In the middle of the road there is a young male walking around in circles and a further casualty lying half on the road with his legs still in the front driver compartment. I get out of our vehicle with the usual feelings of uncertainty and anxiety about the condition of the patients. Already the initial assessment is being made in my mind. The guy walking is still alive and the one in or out of the car appears lifeless and motionless, he is my priority.

There are other people present but I don't ask what happened as this usually causes a rush of information from the most traumatised of those in attendance. I listen carefully to any conversations as I approach the patient, gathering information but focusing on the condition of the driver lying still on the road. I hear a policeman say that he assesses the speed to have been about 70 miles per hour. On this kind of a night and with the road conditions he would never have made the corner safely. The car has been stopped abruptly by the nearby tree. Trees are very unforgiving and this is a very old, and very sturdy looking tree. Seventy miles per hour to zero in a fraction of a second, it is a miracle that the passenger, the one wandering around in circles, is alive never mind mobile. The reason for his good fortune becomes clear on further investigation.

The engine and peddles are crushed into the drivers well and the front of the car does not exist anymore. I bend down to assess the patient feeling for both a radial pulse and carotid. The onlookers, a young couple, say they have pulled him out of the car. This is not always the best policy as it can compromise the condition of any neck or back injury, however people do what they think is best at the time. The couple have been travelling in the same direction and stopped on realisation that the road was blocked.

There is no pulse so I try for a carotid pulse in the neck, still no result. I lean forward to feel for a rise in the chest, then listen and smell for breathing. There is a strong smell of alcohol around the patient and I notice a couple of cans in the foot well of the driver's side of the car. I cannot detect any respiration. Steve, the paramedic appears on my right side with our monitor from the ambulance. The monitor is a very sensitive piece of equipment used to detect and record heartbeat, analyse breathing rates and many other functions including a defibrillator for use when the heart is in chaotic rhythm. I wait for the machine to pick up any response but all that is present are three flat lines.

On further examination I see his pupils are fixed and dilated. His head is resting in a pool of blood. The Paramedic, Steve agrees there is no life sign, he is deceased. At this point another two Paramedics arrive and also confirm life is extinct for the patient on the road.

The other patient, the Circling Male, is taken to the back of the newly arrived ambulance from which the two paramedics had emerged. The young male on the ground is covered up with a blanket from the ambulance. I can feel the trauma from the onlookers from the other car, it is probably the first dead body they have seen, it is not my first experience but for some reason I feel upset in a different way from previous occasions. I don't know why, but there is an atmosphere around this accident.

There are now five police cars in attendance, miles from anywhere and in the middle of the night, it is now one thirty in the morning. The reason for this also becomes clear as the story unfolds.

I notice that there is a huddle of three paramedics and several police officers by the side of the deceased male. My mind is now on the Circling Male, it is best not to get involved with whatever gossip is ensuing over there by the wrecked car. Instead I shall go to the other ambulance to ascertain the needs of the circling male. I climb aboard to find a young female in the back of the ambulance taking the details from the young man. I ask if it is alright if I take a look at his injuries and she agrees with what seems like a sigh of relief. She is a 'first responder' who is trained to work in the community to attend incidents where the patient is experiencing cardiac problems. She is the reason we were given a category 'A' response time. The first responder has already achieved a fourteen minute response, thereby hitting the government targets. Now of course the Service have realised that they can send them to any incident, trained or not, to achieve response times. No figures, no funding, big mistake in policy. How awful it will be if it costs lives. Or do they really care? So this unqualified Lassie has arrived on time, and our response time will not be included in the figures, marvellous!

Back to the job in hand. This young man of twenty years requires hospital treatment. He has head injuries which are distorting his usually bald and smooth head into something that resembles a lumpy pomegranate, same colour at least. He is stinking of alcohol and tells me he was asleep when the accident happened. This is most probably the reason he is alive. He would have been completely relaxed when the car hit the tree. He tells me they are returning home from a bar-b-q to celebrate his friends return from Iraq. The Circling Man tells me he has been a friend to the driver since school days. The Driver is twenty one and has just served six months dodging bullets from insurgents in Basra. Which just goes to prove how dangerous trees are in the middle of the night.

'How is my pal?' I knew that was coming. I did not want to answer. I hate emotional intensities especially if I cannot run away. It seems as clear as daylight what I must tell

him. 'He didn't make it, he's dead'. That's how I handled it,
right or wrong, but I believe pandering around in these
questions only aggravates the outcome. The circling man just
looked at me, no tears, no crying, no shouting just, nothing. I
have never experienced such raw emotion in my life, it is
draining. You need to go to hospital I tell him. He says ok and
nods. The first responder lady looks very pale so I ask her if
she minds if I leave the vehicle to alert the other paramedics
of the need for a run to the hospital. It is then that all the
commotion and attention to this incident becomes clear. The
circling man says his pal is the local policeman's son. He says
the father retired last Friday and was looking forward to his
son's return so they could go fishing tomorrow. How awful is
that! I left the Ambulance to return to the Police Officers who
knew the dead boy personally, and of course, his dad too. So
this is the reason for the all out response and our being
guided into the accident by control, to avoid delay. It is just
human nature to move mountains when one of your own
requires assistance.

I approach the Ambulance Officers who arrived later
in their vehicle and now have the Circling Male on board. I
mention that in my opinion the 'laddie' needs hospital
treatment and they say 'Are you taking him or do we have to'.
Sometimes I can't believe the attitude of some of my
colleagues. 'He's in your vehicle' I say 'and therefore your
patient, plus I have some forms to fill out'. We have to
complete a 'recognition of death' form and pass the paper
work to the Police on these occasions. I have to admit I am a
wee bit wound up that they even considered our taking the

'Circling Male' in our vehicle, it is just pure laziness on their part as they wish to go back and put their feet up. Vocational dedication can be evaporated over years of Management expectation that we are super human, it can develop into creating worn out, long serving Paramedics.

The paper work takes a while as the Police have to do a little bit of digging to find out the proper name of the deceased male driver. Dates of birth and address also cause a problem but the Police Officers put down the fathers details in order that we can be on our way. It would be wrong to tie up an Ambulance for any length of time as we may be required elsewhere and our skills are no longer needed here.

I complete the forms with the Sergeant and Inspector on scene and we bid our farewells, pack up the gear and tidy the Ambulance to be ready for the next job after a cuppa back at the Station. We are told to return to base by control.

Forty Two

CHAPTER – AMBLE

The drive back is relaxed and at a sensible speed. It is a time to reflect on the job we have completed. We reflect on the senselessness of the loss of life and the tragic circumstances of the drivers return from Iraq. To dodge bullets for six months only to be put to rest by a combination of Alcohol and Nature. How sad is that? We both agree.

Tiredness sets in, it's a very dark night, with cloud covering the stars and moon. We have travelled for around fifty minutes when something catches our attention in the headlights of our vehicle. Something resting against a tree, it could be a car so we slow down for a better look. The tree is on the roadside next to a path leading into Amble and on the other side of the path are woods. There is very little light but I spot movement in the woods and ask the driver Steve, to stop. I am still the attendant and would like a closer look. There appears to be someone crawling along the ground and flopping down into the grass every few seconds.

I ask Steve to stay in the Ambulance and inform Control while I take a closer look. He presses the radio button to alert Control as to why we are stopping. This is necessary as they monitor the vehicles movement at all times. I go for the vehicle's battery torch but it is not working, so I revert to my pen torch and the side floods of the vehicle. The object which I thought rested against the tree is I realise, a car, not resting but wrapped around the tree like a scarf. Inside the wreckage is a young male, upright and motionless. It almost looks like he is strapped to the tree as a punishment. As I approach I see he is still tied to the wreckage by his seat belt. His eyes are open and staring so I call out to him even though my senses tell me he is dead. I approach him with stealth. I try to find a carotid pulse but there is none. I call to Steve that we have a major problem here and we may need help. There are two patients whether deceased or not.

Leaving the car and the upright male, I go over to the fence where I saw the initial crawling figure. As I climb over the fence I call to him. As I near the crawling figure I realise he is only a wee lad of about fourteen his head covered in blood. I ask him what has happened but he doesn't respond, only cries and groans. He is covered in blood around his head so I get a little closer in case he has not heard me properly. I ask again what has happened but this time with specific questions. Has he been hit by the car? He says his feet hurt, so I look down to find he has no shoes on and his feet look dirty and are also covered in blood. I ask if he has he been assaulted by anyone, no reply. The incidents may not be related, but this would be unlikely. I am working in the dark, and I don't like black woods at night at the best of times. I realise I need some equipment from the snatch bag that we carry in the ambulance. I quickly run back to fetch it from the cab and at the same time update Steve in case he has missed any of my observations.

As I am returning to the crawling male a car draws up and a young male jumps out shouting abuse. Whether at me or the Crawling Male, I have no idea but I don't like this bloke's attitude, so I respond with similar flowery language asking him to 'be quiet please'! I ask him to turn his car round to face the woods so as to create more light and much to my surprise he immediately obliges.

I am returning to the crawling male when suddenly I am aware of groaning noises emanating from further into the woods. I am back in the dark, so I use the pen torch but it's too dark to see anything clearly and quite frightening not knowing what or who I may encounter. I spin around to look further into the woods and right there in my face is another male.

Not the Groaning Male, not the Crawling Male but another one altogether, standing, his pale face reflected by the headlights of the car. It is likening something out of a horror movie with bodies popping up from all over. I have to admit I am terrified by this guy but I keep composure because that's what we do isn't it! He is shorter than me and maybe about fifteen years old. I don't see any obvious injuries and he is standing so I tell him to stay put and not move a muscle until I get help for him. Once again I shout to Steve about this new development.

The upright male, the Crawling Male, the Groaning Male, the Pale Faced Zombie, what next? I tread carefully into the woods with my pen torch praying the triple 'A' batteries hold out for a wee while longer. I weave my way between the trees in the direction of the groaning sounds which from time to time turn to a noise like a screaming banshee, not that I have ever heard one. There appears to be several branches lying around which seem as if they are recently torn from their parent bodies by the fresh sap look that wood has when you cut a branch from a tree. I can see movement about 10 yards ahead. There is a male lying on the ground writhing to the rhythm of every stabbing pain his body is encountering. I have to approach with caution as he thrashes out with his legs and arms as his head rises from the ground to reveal his facial injuries. His mouth opens wide as he screams in agony, spraying blood over his jacket and hands which he tries to hold up to his face but doesn't seem to quite manage to reach. That screaming, as I will find out later, will not leave my head and will return in the future without warning triggered by many different scenarios, noises and sights.

I lean towards him and try to pass his flailing limbs then I am met with his face in mine and he lets out a deathly scream in my face, followed by the spray of blood from his injuries. Suddenly at my back is Frankie, a friend in the service who works for a different department that transfers patients from hospital to hospital. I ask him where he came from and he says he was just passing and stopped to give a hand. Steve appears right behind him followed by a Police Officer.

We all pounce on the Thrashing Male and try to hold him down to assess his injuries. We manage to stop him kicking and punching us as we all take a limb and a further Police Officer arrives to help, who holds his middle to stop him writhing around but to no avail, the Thrashing Male is too far gone to know what is happening and cannot be controlled for more than a few seconds. I get the first Officer to hold both legs as I return to the ambulance for the back board and some straps to tie him down and return to the scene. We try again but once again he is too agitated to restrain. Back to the ambulance again but this time for the Vac Mat. An invaluable piece of equipment that wraps around the patient. By this time those holding him down are tiring and beg for me to be quick, or words to that effect. The air is sucked out of the vac mat and it hardens around the patient like a rock. We manage to get it under him somehow. Everybody is shouting suggestions to each other in order to be heard above the screams of the Thrashing Male and eventually we are successful enough to secure him, but we are all covered in bruises by now. We carry him like a body in a sack back to the ambulance. Unfortunately that is just what he turns out to be the next day.

I notice that from the time I started my search for the Groaning Male who, subsequently turns into the Thrashing Male, there have been developments behind me at this scene of carnage. There are another three ambulances arriving, several police cars and two fire engines on scene. Apparently it has been fifteen minutes since I found the Thrashing Male and we all piled in to him, with compassion of course. As the Paramedics disembarked I allocated one crew to the Crawling Male and one to the Spooky Zombie.

It is only at this moment that one of the other crews from Belford headed by my pal Coogie, notices a further male, number five, trapped in the boot of the wreck which is wrapped around the tree. He seems barely alive so Coogie takes this one as his patient and I return to the Trashing Male who is now on board our vehicle and we need to leave immediately to get him to the nearest hospital eight miles down the road.

I am the attendant but opt to drive as my partner is a Paramedic and is able to cannulate the laddie to access IV treatment on route or at least prepare him as best as possible for the staff at the hospital. I jump in the driver's seat and radio to Control to alert the hospital of a teenage male with multiple injuries and a combative nature that we will need to be met at the casualty doors with a trauma team.

The Thrashing Male never let up all the way to the hospital. Frankie and Steve both had to virtually sit on him to keep him from harming himself and also themselves in the process. IV access was impossible for the lads in the back, firstly because the Thrashing Male was thrashing and also because we needed to get to hospital as fast as possible and, all one can do at ninety miles per hour in the back of an ambulance is to hang on and pray, oh, and trust the driver, but that is something I do very well.

It took us about six minutes to do the eight miles as it is fairly straight road all the way to the hospital with only a couple of roundabouts. On our arrival there is a team standing outside the hospital. It must be about four in the morning now and the adrenaline has kept us going for the last hour. There are two nurses and two Doctors awaiting our arrival, one male and three females. I jump out of the driver's seat and go around to back of the vehicle, open the doors, retract the lift and release the stretcher. It is very difficult to keep the Thrashing Male on the stretcher even though he is trapped and tied into the Vac Mattress, but with all our strength we manage with Steve, Franky and I to get the stretcher off the Ambulance and into the trauma room.

Now the real fight starts as we lift him onto the hospital cot and we have to release him from the Vac Mat to allow access for the doctors to his arms and legs. He needs 'calm you down' drugs right now to give him a chance.

It is only now that I get a good look at his head injuries in the cold light of the trauma room. He has several around the cranium some of which reveal matter from within, it's no wonder he is combative and disturbed as he must have intracranial bleeding causing pressure within the skull. Steve and Frankie leave the room to clear up the back of the vehicle while I stay with my patient after the handover to assist with the securing of the patient. It's a messy affair, we are all being whacked by the fists and feet of the thrashing male but eventually after about thirty minutes we have cannulas in his arms and the drugs to tranquilise him take effect.

I am thanked by the trauma staff for my assistance and I leave to get some fresh air and to help clean the equipment. It is now about five in the morning and I still have not had that cuppa.

I hear later from the scene of accident Officers that is the worst incident they have had to deal with in the last twenty years. The Fire Brigade Officers are all debriefed when they return to the Station in Amble, the same night. The Police have a similar process in place for their Officers. The Ambulance Service have nothing in place. Outside I am met by the staff support representative, who is really just another Paramedic with minimal insight into the art of counselling. He asks me if I'm ok and for the first time in three years on the road as a fully qualified Advance Technician I reply 'No I want taken off the road I've had enough tonight'. To this he agrees and scurries off to inform Control.

However life isn't as simple and when I call control to tell them I'm off home having finished cleaning the vehicle in preparation for the next shift, I am asked if I am ready for the next job. My answer to that is no as I have seen too many young lives wasted on this shift. I went home thinking this was an end to a hard nights work but I was not to know what was coming.

Forty Three

THE CONSEQUENCES

That night, or day, brought little sleep as every time I closed my eyes I could see the Thrashing Male screaming in my face, the Zombie lad, pale faced just staring at me not a word said by him, the Crawling Male with his hand raised up as if pleading for help and the wreck of the car with the standing male wrapped up as if in a spiders web waiting for his captor to descend and devour him. To this day I still see them clearly as if it had happened last night, sometimes they are dismissed from my mind and at other times they get into my psyche and the consequence are the symptoms of Post Traumatic Stress Disorder.

The next few days were bizarre with heightening feelings of anxiety but I returned to work on the Tuesday and lo and behold what did we get called to but another car accident. I was again the attendant as I was working at another Station on relief for someone off on the sick. The accident was at low speed thankfully and the injuries were minor although we put the patient on a Spinal Board as a precaution with a collar and took him to hospital as he complained of neck pain. He was actually quite a decent bloke and we had a good laugh on the way to the hospital. He had insisted on his mobile phone coming with him so we put it between his legs for safe keeping. I told him if he put it on vibrate it would keep his mind off his neck pain.

I believe matters were worsened by the total lack of compassion shown by the Management and Control three days after the Amble incident when I was giving my statement to the Police.

The Officer arrives on Station to take my statement about the incident for which I am given half an hour to complete by Control. I inform the officer Steve Armstrong that I have had difficulty over the past three days trying to come to terms with the consequences of the incident. Notably, the daytime visions and nightmares of the night in Amble Woods. He tells me to take my time as he needs a comprehensive statement of the incident in case it comes to court at a later date. I begin with chapter one and continue through to chapter two but not without extreme anxiety as I recall each and every detail. It is not a difficult scenario as I have already written the whole incident down on paper. It is part of my twelve step AA program to write all memories and emotional difficulties down and share them with another human being who fully understands. The Officer in question works in the traffic division and has a good understanding and vast experience of the difficulties of recalling stressful incidents such as these.

However the process becomes very intense as Control calls in the middle of my recounting my experiences, insisting that I terminate the statement and ask the Police Officer to come back later for completion. I say no to this request which is a brave thing to do as Control like to live up to their name, and do just that, Control. I explain that this is too traumatic an experience to interrupt and may be detrimental to my state of mind if I stop at this point. To this they reply that I will do as I am told and have my lunch break now and be ready for the road in half an hour. I once again refused this request and tell them I will complete the Statement.

At this juncture the Paramedic Station Officer with whom I am partnered for this day shift decides to chip in and endorsed the orders from Control. I inform him of my worsening state of mind and tell him to back off, which he does and scuttles off to inform Control of the situation. He always has been enthusiastic to inform on his colleagues. I can feel my emotions and anxiety rising in intensity as I continue speaking to Steve the Traffic Officer. He senses this and gives me his contact number in case I need any witness to this ridicules situation. He recalls that he has never been so disgusted with the treatment of a witness giving a statement to such a traumatic incident. Especially as this is the Ambulance Service and one would imagine they should embrace some sort of compassion and understanding.

I finish the statement eventually in-between choking back the tears and repeated stops for composure. The Officer leaves and I am left in the Station feeling tired and emotional with only the company of a heartless boss, who is still going on about my 'duty' and it is the 'nature of the job'. I agree it is the nature of the job and that should be recognised by the Service.

I call Control and tell them I am going home as I am not fit enough to continue through stress caused by the behaviour of both the Station Officer and Control and add that I feel they have shown no compassion for my condition.

To this day I still have no support from the Service only aggravation and harassment up to now. Their answer to my problem is to dismiss me on the grounds of ill health and they refuse to acknowledge responsibility for my condition of Post Traumatic Stress Disorder. The condition has been confirmed by a Consultant Psychiatrist, the Occupational Health Doctor for the Service and my own GP who all agree that the PTSD is as a result of the Sharperton and Amble Incidents.

My application for ill health has been completed by the Human Resource Department who refuse to acknowledge that the condition is caused by work related incidents. I feel I have been dismissed for performing my duty.

Forty Four

JOURNEY TO THE HEARING.

After the incident with control I went home and I made an appointment with my local General Practitioner (GP). I have always had an inherent fear of Doctors, nurtured over the years most likely from my frequent visits to alleviate my symptoms of active Alcoholism. GP's are less than happy to have an active addict sitting opposite them in their surgeries. The powerlessness they experience over such an illness I would imagine is very frustrating. It had been suggested on more than one occasion what my problem stemmed from but was in no good frame of mind to listen. I believe GP's are trained to diagnose and find a solution to Physical and mental maladies. Alcoholism carries with it a further complication of a spiritual void for the sufferer. For this the GP has no answer or certainly not one the patient is willing to accept.

I shall return to the fact that I am an Alcoholic as it has a very significant impact on the Post Traumatic Stress Disorder diagnosis about to be bestowed upon me by the GP, Consultant Psychiatrist and the Occupational Health Doctor at the Ambulance HQ .

As I have intimated the Doctors waiting room is not a place that endears me to rational thinking at the best of times, but I was desperate and felt that my head would explode at any given moment.

I paced the floor at home for many a hour wanting to pick up the phone and ask for help, while at the same time full of fear at the consequence of such a monumental act, but pick it up I did, thank God.

Much to my relief and surprise the respondent at the other end of the line was helpful and maybe understanding, well certainly the first. She offered me an appointment the very next day as I said it was a matter of urgency.

I phoned Kari, my Wife, to tell her what had happened and she intimated that the Control were parentless, with the suggestion that they were also fornicating. Kari always has had a way of thoroughly explaining the situation in the shortest pathway possible. She also has a sharp intuition for my feelings.

As I sat in the Doctors waiting room I imagined all the responses I would receive from the GP, from pull yourself together to committing me to an asylum for 28 days. I have been less than anxious to attend the GP's surgery in the past and on this occasion the intensity of my feelings put me in a very vulnerable state of mind.

I did not have to wait long fortunately, but the walk to the surgery door, all of about thirty meters seemed like a mile and yet I wished it were longer to steady my mind. I had been rehearsing what I would say when I sat in the patients chair.

Would he think I was a fraud like many other people who attend an appointment in order to have a few sick days off because the weather is good?

Would he understand what it had been like for me in the past days? After all he's not in my mind. I had begun to isolate myself. I did not want burden my family with these intrusive images of the lad with the pulped head and mouth screaming in my face, with the blood emerging from his mouth like one of those spray guns you use for foliage in the house. The lad who was tied into the wreckage by the metal shards of the high performance car, his lifeless face and the touch of his cold skin on my hand as I tried to detect life in his listless body.

I knocked on the door and entered the Doctor's consulting room. He invited me to sit in the patient's chair and asked how he could be of help. I was unable to answer for a few moments as I felt the pressure inside my whole persona about to explode and I cried for the first time in my life in front of a stranger.

I have heard it said that the relief of such an experience is very therapeutic but I found no evidence to support that theory on this occasion. I felt very vulnerable, ashamed and defenceless.

The Doctor told me to take my time and I remember thinking 'right that is exactly what I will do', and spent the next 30 minutes revealing the incidents, my feelings during and after and how I could not go back to work in my present condition. He was very understanding and seemed to fully comprehend the intensity of my situation. He signed me off for four weeks and instructed me to make another appointment to review my symptoms.

I went off with stress. I had no idea of the seriousness of my condition and the implications about to enfold.

I went to an Alcoholics Anonymous (AA) meeting that evening, to speak to my friends in the fellowship. It is the only therapy for the illness of Alcoholism that has worked for me to date, for the past eighteen years. I had tried all the other therapies including clinics in Scotland, cutting down, harm reduction, self will, and many others too numerous to mention. AA is the only therapeutic treatment for my alcoholism that has worked for me on a daily basis. It has a support network all over the world and is free, apart for our own contributions.

When I left the Doctor's surgery armed with a diagnosis of severe stress I went home to inform the NEAS of the situation, fully expecting some understanding and compassion which might lighten the heavy burden laid upon me by the effects of my experiences.

However this is not what transpired which left me feeling alone and abandoned.

The Manager never contacted me for a month and then only to ask when am I coming back to work. No indication of 'how are you' or 'can we help in any way', just a demand, which I was to learn was the first step to initiating my dismissal.

This career has been the only one to give me a feeling of inner self worth and purpose, only to be destroyed by the ensuing process of heartless intervention by the NEAS.

I went for help from my union, Unison, who washed their hands of the whole affair when I mentioned the possibility of challenging the NEAS in court for wrongful dismissal.

I tried several firms of solicitors but they all ran for cover when I mentioned PTSD. They all said that they were fearful of going to court as they would inevitably lose as it would set a precedent to rule in favour of wrongful dismissal which would in turn open the floodgates to all those suffering from the disease in the Emergency Services and the Armed Forces. So help and understanding became a lost cause, but I fought on because I hate injustice and I am stupid and stubborn. I fought the case alone against two NEAS Barristers and their lawyer. Needless to say I lost but gained a moral victory with my face all over the local papers which was a victory to some degree.

However the consequence was I lost my family and marriage and am now left alone at 65 years of age with a feeling of rejection and failure.

<u>This is a copy of the letter to a Tribunal held as a consequence
to the lack of support by the NEAS</u>

Dear Sir or madam,

I am disabled by the illness of PTSD.

I feel panic and fear while I write this testimony.

I am persistently required to prove my disability without treatment to individuals who may or may not understand the full impact of PTSD on my everyday life.

I therefore would ask that you keep in mind that this testimony is given after treatment and that my condition would be far graver if that were not the case.

Without treatment I would have been unable to attend any Tribunals or assessment interviews. I cast aside my own welfare and on occasions, the wellbeing of my family to pursue these unwanted pressures.

A lay person may expect compassion to be shown for a person suffering from the illness of PTSD. However this is not my experience as explained in my testimony. I feel the situation and my illness have been further exacerbated by the attitude and behaviour of my former employers, the Ambulance Service (AS) NHS Trust.

If my physical appearance today was without an eye, leg or arm, the proof of my disability would be visually evident. I have none of these obvious infirmities. My disability is only evident by my attitudes, behaviour and mental stability on a day to day basis.

I have continually given statements about my illness and the disabling effect it has had upon my life to many differing agencies. I have further been raped of my dignity by the persistent requests for personal medical reports and the release of my medical records to complete strangers.

I cannot transfer my feelings, thoughts or physical malady to any other human being, or, the mental anguish this has caused both me and my family. I can only relate these experiences to you today in the hope that it will go in some way to help the reader understand. I will endeavour to convey and communicate the suffering and pain which is inherent with the illness of PTSD.

I am an honest man and live an honest program in all my affairs, excluding none. I have learned this through the programme of Alcoholics Anonymous. I have been a member of this organisation for the past twenty five years.

The symptoms of the illnesses of PTSD and Alcoholism are experienced not only by the individual, but they also affect the whole family.

I mention this here as my Alcoholism and addiction to mind altering drugs prevents me from taking the suggested medication for the PTSD condition.

The issues considered here are about me personally and relate to no other individual. However I feel my experience reflects the needs of all Emergency Services Personnel who may suffer from this disabling illness of PTSD in the future.

There is no appropriate help (fit for the purpose) or any system of support in place for any of Emergency Ambulance Service workers, when considering the illness of PTSD. This is despite the Ambulance Service being aware of the problem for a number of years. However at an Employment Tribunal the AS said they were unaware of the existence of this illness in their Staff.

There is no immediate care provision available from the NHS for this illness, as stated in the initial report on me by a

Consultant Psychiatrist. For this reason I accessed my CBT and specialist PTSD counselling privately for two years.

In the Ambulance Services there seems only expectation that the individual should carry out their duty uninformed of the psychological dangers. The nature of this work environment is one in which the individual hides their fears and feelings from their employers and work colleagues. It is a very 'Macho' environment. There was inadequate content about these dangers in the training program provided by the AS. Nothing pointed to the Psychological eventualities of exposure to witnessing persistent and regular trauma. In my experience the AS has no support network, which was fit for the purpose.

No person likes to think they are Physically, Mentally or Spiritually different from their fellow humans. Therefore it is not surprising that over the past few years while suffering from PTSD have been characterised by vain attempts at being normal.

The idea that one day I will be able to control the symptoms of PTSD has become an obsession resulting in abnormality. The persistence of this illusion has taken me to the gates of insanity and close to death. I am told by my therapists that the delusion that I am now like other people has to be cast aside. The acceptance of my disability is the first step to a solution of this possibly permanent condition.

I now realise after experiencing the symptoms for almost ten years that the PTSD may and most probably will be permanent with no cure, but, there can be temporary respite from the symptoms.

I am like a man who has lost his legs. He cannot grow new ones. This man is disabled.

Part of my neural functioning has altered. It has ceased to function normally. I cannot grow a new one. I am disabled concerning many day to day tasks. It has been proved that the ACC part of the brain changes when individuals develop PTSD. I have researched and found proof of the dysfunction, from articles and research from various sources. They all refer to Emergency Services Personnel.

PTSD is a very serious illness and can affect the sufferer for long periods of time on a day to day basis. The intensity of the symptoms fluctuates, but the memories are always there. With therapy I may not react so much to the symptoms. I will never live a normal life again. I accept that today I am changed by my experiences.

One of the common symptoms of this illness is alcohol and substance abuse. As mentioned above I am also a recovering Alcoholic/Addict and have been clean and sober for the past 25 years and through this experience of recovery I joined the Ambulance service to make a difference. I expected in my innocence that such a professional organisation would care for the welfare of the carer. Without the Fellowship of AA I would not have survived the experience... The meetings and sharing have been my one of the most productive therapies in dealing with the symptoms of PTSD.

I was never made aware when joining the Ambulance Service, or at any time thereafter, that witnessing traumatic events could make me susceptible to the symptoms of PTSD. However I believe that the AS must have been aware of the dangers of continual exposure to such traumatic incidents. The Ambulance Services across the world have been aware of this for at least 15 years and more.

Today I am still unable to work as an employee. At times it doesn't feel like I am worth anything. I am continually questioned and doubted about my illness of PTSD, which makes me feel I am not believed. My faith in God and the support of my family and friends in the AA Fellowship help tremendously. However the illness took me to rock bottom and I experienced the futility of existence. I felt isolated. I was ready to take my own life.

I know that you cannot see inside my head it is not made of glass. The only way of communicating the intensity of this illness is by my own verbal testament.

I am not a seasoned advocate and do not profess to be one. I can only put myself at the mercy of the reader in the hope that you will understand the anguish and pain of this illness.

By bringing the case against the AS I hoped the AS may be required to implement health and safety precautions within their policies to protect their workers from further damage and possible dismissal if the workers develop PTSD while in their employ.

Reports from my GP, Consultant Psychiatrist, PTSD Therapist and the Occupational Health Doctor for the AS confirmed my condition and state of disability. Along with the statements from my Wife, a colleague and my own personal testament about the day to day effects on my everyday life, and the subsequent detrimental changes to the relationships within my personal life.

I became ill through my job and because of this the AS sacked me for being disabled.

A Tribunal heard the evidence and they agreed that I should have been sacked for being disabled.

However I feel I lost the case as my adversaries were all seasoned Barristers and I was indeed lost in the jungle of legal jargon, but there were no legal teams who would assist me in my defence, I think through fear of losing.

I leave you to come to your own conclusions!

Forty Five
Gran Canaria - The first year

Why did we come to live here? That in itself is a peculiar journey. It all started with a desire for change. Not spoken of but felt by both Karen, who has been my soul mate for the past fifteen years, and myself. Oh yes, and the terrorist bombers in Sharm el Sheik that facilitated a twist in our fortunes. However, that initial spark which gave us the courage to change came from the adrenaline junky within us both, the desire to escape the mundane. It is not until you cut the chains that you realise just how tied you are to the illusion of security whist living in a cage. Ask the animals at any zoo!

We were full of anticipation about our new adventure. It was 13.15pm and the plane circled Las Palmas. The aircraft made the usual bumpy approach due to the permanent cross winds experienced at Gran Canarias's main airport.

Our new home, Kari, Alisha, our six year old daughter, and I, exchanged relieved glances as it had been a rocky few days in our build up to our new life. The house sale falling through at the last moment being the main concern but over that we were powerless, we just had to be resolved to start again with the search for a buyer for the bungalow in Widdrington, Northumberland. The H–Browns who pulled out of the sale at the very last minute took some stick in our thoughts that week and our wishes for them were not entirely Christian, or built on spiritual guidelines. Or maybe they were, as Hell seemed a suitable destination for their souls at that point, however it was not good for our Karma. Maybe illustrated by what happened over the next few weeks.

The aeroplane circled for it's final approach, only a couple of hundred feet to go and we were on Gran Canaria, finally, our new resting place for the future. The aircraft suddenly veered off to the right and started to ascend, quickly. Now I don't know if you have ever experienced the unthinkable but it is amazing how quickly we can go from relaxed complacency to blind anxiety in a split second.

Another plane had been taking off as we were landing. 'Not unusual for Gran Canaria' were the pilot's words. Oh joy! But I suppose you are nearer to God in the sky. We three all exchanged similar glances expressing thoughts of 'Oh my God what are we doing? First suicide bombers and now near misses! I have come to believe that we should be aware of 'signs' in our lives as to our destination and follow them. However it appears that on this occasion, I would have to put them down as testers of our determination to succeed in our new adventure.

Safely landed after the second attempt and a few sighs of relief from our fellow passengers, we disembarked to retrieve the suitcases and collect our hire car. Oh, and Kari puked all over the disabled toilet on landing, but that is not particularly unusual!

We were booked into a hotel in the south of the Island called the Club Puerto Atlantico, owned by an interesting, but not so colourful German character who's business was linked to a dodgy holiday club purchase we had made on a previous visit to Gran Canaria. Gullible, certainly not, we had our wits about us all the time we were being ripped off.

Mr Keiser, the owner, had invented a Holiday Club called Design Vacations. We had bought into it at a cost of 5665 Euros, a weak moment in our lives while relaxed on holiday. The guy who actually conned us into the enterprise went by the name of Kevan Hammell who I later found out had ripped off most of the island residents along with the tourists. Was that his real name? I still don't know today but he had been a window salesman in the UK and he was running from his debtors. He eventually took refuge in the Canaries as had hundreds of other criminals.

Looking back, this scam was quite fascinating as it developed, it sucked us in and spat us out like naive children who had never heard of such a thing before, which of course we had, and previously vowed in front of a witnessing television, in the comfort of our own home, 'we would never do that, those people must be so stupid.' But we were stupid! Don't ask me why! I still cannot believe we parted with our money to a con man, but we did, just as many other thousands of tourists have done over the last few years. About 400,000 to date I believe, just in the UK alone. Good honest people with hard earned cash conned by dishonest thieves with no conscience.

How were we booked into this Crook's hotel? Well, we had been given a free holiday voucher for one week through the scam. It was another opportunity for the operators of these scams to further relieve us of our hard earned cash as the hotel sported a couple of dozen time share apartments, and

reps. "Danger Mr. Robinson aliens in human disguise".
However, we were now aware and had turned this to our
own good advantage. We had used it to secure our first week
in Gran Canaria. It would give us time to settle in, buy a car
and rent a flat. Sounds easy, but proved to be a little more
difficult than we first imagine.

It was very hot. We had arrived at the start of a Calima. A
condition derived from the hot winds in the Sahara Desert
which is only 150 Miles away in Africa. The temperature
soared to a sticky fifty degrees and we had no air conditioning
in the apartment. Nice place we had chosen for our new
home. Why Gran Canaria, we still don't know, it just
happened, OK.

The hotel had a lovely pool and was right on the rocks which
afforded us a beautiful view of the Atlantic Ocean and at dusk
the most wonderful sunsets you could imagine. The
apartment we were in thanks to the time share con we fell
for, was very comfortable apart from the heat which we were
not used to. The room had no air conditioning but I think that
probably helped us acclimatise to our future five years on the
Island.

I am a sucker for sunsets and sunrises, they seem to take
away all the crap out of my head, and I had my fair share of
that from experiences in the Ambulance Service as a
Paramedic. Over time I had developed Post Traumatic Stress
Disorder, More of that later as there was still a lot of settling
down to do in our new homeland.

Can you believe that we were fluent in the Spanish language?
Yes we knew about four or five words between us. ''Hola' we

said to the concierge, the room maid, the taxi driver and anybody else who looked Spanish. 'Hola' they said back mistaking us for tourists. No, we have come to live here and we are one of you now. How naive we were in the beginning. 'Gracias' was our second word which we banded around as if we were fluent. We didn't know it was a dead giveaway as the Canarians do not pronounce their words the same as the mainland Spaniards.

We enjoyed two full weeks in the apartments and made the most of the time planning where we were to live. We eventually found a flat in the northern end of the island where we spent two months before deciding it was too windy up there and moved south to the tourist area and the sunshine and beaches.

Karen's job and Alisha's school were one and the same. Collegio Arenas. A private fee paying school near San Fernando.

Here is where it all went wrong. Karen and Alisha lasted four days at the school before finding out it was not the place it seemed. Karen resigned and we needed to find a new place for Alisha.

I had problems with my PTSD condition and the whole thing seemed as if it would go tits up. Not a good start to our new lives, it appeared one thing after another fell apart before we could get started.

We were desperate and in a foreign country where we could not speak the language. It had been a tough journey with many disappointments along the way but we learned to think on our feet. I have always loved the saying, 'if you want to give God a laugh tell him your plans!!!'

Forty Six

I met a guy in AA on the island who worked for a company selling time share. Although I had heard the horror stories about the business and experienced the consequences first hand, I walked into the holiday complex and asked for a job. After an interview they said they would give me the training and a three month contract to see if my face fitted in the team and also to find out if I could con the public without a conscience.

Now that is not easy to do when you have learned to live an honest program in your life.

We moved Alisha from the Spanish private school to the British School of Gran Canaria. Karen was offered a temporary job there after about two months while I worked at Anfi del Mar selling dreams to the poor unsuspecting tourists often asking them to part with 12000 pounds upwards for the privilege of one week of holiday per year. It amazes me how many people fall for the Con, including myself or course.

I lasted the three months then got my marching orders as I did not have the ability to fit into the team of cocaine addicts, alcoholics and just plain dishonest men and women who just loved to succeed for the sake of feeding their habits.

I felt a great sense of relief as I walked away knowing I did not have to fulfil obligations that were contrary to my nature.

I started to advertise my counselling skills which eventually brought in a couple of hundred Euros a month, so along with Karen's part time teaching and private tuition we managed to afford an apartment overlooking the sea. The sun sets were truly amazing but the place was overrun with cockroaches. We only stayed there for a few months before buying a house in a complex with a pool.

The people who lived there were mainly Spanish and Norwegian, sixteen villas in all and also overlooking the sea. Things settled down after our initial traumas and we secured a mortgage to buy the house which was put in Karen's name to avoid complications due to inheritance tax, if one of us popped our clogs. I can see today that once again my good trusting nature cost me everything as I signed away all rights to a woman who in the near future deserted me and took everything including my most precious gift from God, Alisha our daughter.

Trust is a vital part of any relationship but it has to come from both parties. I have been too trusting as far as partners are concerned in my life and now find issues of trust in relationships very difficult. In fact impossible, I cannot let anyone close to me any more for the fears I carry, however more of that later.

I met some wonderful people on Gran Canaria through my counselling clients and AA.

I cannot mention names for reasons of confidentiality. But I can relate some of the situations that brought my clients to my door.

One was a Sergeant at Arms for a Hells Angels gang in Holland but found it increasingly difficult to function as the Cocaine and Alcohol took over his daily life. His partner and mother of his children also became a client through Heroin and Alcohol dependence. They both became clean and sober and as far as

I know at the time of writing they are still free from their addictions. They run a tattoo and alternative health clinic on the island.

I also had the privilege to be introduce to a pretty young mother of a two year old who is today a counsellor helping addict torn families but not before she burned the house down almost killing herself and the toddler. I and her friends and family helped her access a rehab after leaving the island. Another client fell backwards off a wall after consuming copious amounts of alcohol. He fractured his skull and suffers severe mental problems on a daily basis.

There were many relationship problems that came to me for help. Most of them found the courage to move on from the destructive situation they had built for themselves.

These experiences have convinced me that if a relationship is truly broken then it can never be fixed. Although many of them have formed new relationships and friendships with the same person but none of them stayed together.

But let's be clear about this, there is no helping an unwilling client. I cannot change a person against their will as they will be of the same opinion still!

When we first landed in the canaries the economy was fairly healthy and the cost of living was a third of that in the UK in 2006.

Petrol came at half the cost and there was no road tax. This was all included in the insurance which was also half for the equivalent cover in the UK.

The MOT, which went by the name of CT (don't remember the translation) was a process likened to a car wash. You drove in one end and waited for a guy to check the lights, then drove on to have the underside and brakes checked. If all was well they gave you a piece of paper to cover your car for the next year. Very easy process and fairly inexpensive. Food also came at a third of the cost in the Spanish supermarkets, but not in the tourist stores where the prices were more than in the UK.

I enjoyed the weekends when we changed our clothes and pretended to be tourists. Friday night all the families met on the beach for a picnic about seven o'clock and a swim in the sea.

Saturday, we walked to the other beach for a sandwich and a swim at the tourist resort of Anfi del Mar. Sunday we posed as hotel guests in the Five Star resorts and used their pools and spas.

All in all it was a very different way of life and much more relaxed than the British method of timing everything down to a second. If you were late in the Canaries then you were on time!! Took a bit of getting used to but in the end I think it is better to arrange a time and stick to it. I was always taught that it was rude and disrespectful to be late.

You may think we were now done with falling to scams in the Canaries, but no, we fell as victims to another before we left which we are still owed 3000 Euros today.

We were looking for a new house in the mountains, and discovered that Karen's boss had their Finca up for sale. A Finca is a farm house building, with a small or large piece of land attached.

Most of the mountain dwellings did not have proper planning permission but if the build had been up for more than four years without objection, then it was assumed to be legal. This was the case for the Head Teacher's property but they said they would apply for legal documents just to make sure so I gave them a deposit of 3000 Euros.

Time dragged by and it became evident that the planning papers were not going to appear any day soon. I confronted the owners and they said it would be up to me to apply. Not what we had originally agreed but I conceded, only to be told we could not apply until we became the owners. Stalemate, so I asked for my money back which was met with unwarranted aggression.

I tried on several occasions to confront the owner but he told me he would shoot me if I came back to the property. He was a crazy Canarian and I was advised that if I took it to court it would cost me more than the deposit with a 9o % chance I would lose the court battle because I was an in-comer.

So some things you just have to take on the chin, but what goes around comes around.

We were resident five years on the island and left to go to France for a new adventure.

However the logistics of leaving the island are more complicated than just getting on a plane.

Karen fell out with her boss who had ripped us off and took her to court for harassment but in the end lost the case as Karen left the island to go to the UK with Alisha. They were there for a year while I refurbished the French house as it was not habitable and would have been difficult for us all to live there while the work was in progress.

The house in the Canaries also had to be sold so I stayed on the island to clear up the mess as usual while Karen and Alisha furthered their career and education, living the life of Riley and defrauding the DHSS claiming benefits for a fictional marriage separation, which in the end turned out to be reality.

The house eventually sold but not before I had been traumatised by a dog attack on my legs while I was wandering down the road to sign the transfer papers for the sale. I ended up in hospital with lacerations to both my legs. The pain was quite excruciating.

My family and I have always been dog lovers. We had Boxer dogs as pets for twenty years and I had never been bitten in my life until I was bitten by the next door neighbour's sheep dog while in Widdrington and then again this time on Gran Canaria, also by a sheep dog. I must smell like a Ram. I was of course born in April so I should have known by my star sign!! After all the signing for the house with the new Norwegian owners I was ready to leave. I had arranged for a firm to move our goods and chattels to France which was a wee bit more complicated than I expected as there was customs forms to complete both through the Canarian authorities and the French customs.

Now I was ready to go on the next episode of our world-wide adventure.

<u>Letter to AA Share Magazine from Gran Canaria.</u>

Hi friends, I am an Alcoholic. Sorry it has been so long. I have taken nineteen years to write to Share. Loads of excuses, but none of them hold water, so apologies will have to suffice. I am inspired by the stories and honest sharing in your magazine.

My story!!!!!!!!!!!!!!!! Would you like me to tell my story? Oops big mistake. Once I start I never stop. So here is the edited version that will keep the Grandkids awake at night. I was born in Edinburgh and I still feel deeply that Edinburgh and Scotland are my home. It always will be despite my departure 35 years ago. I had my first proper drink of Alcohol at 14. Two cans of beer. I hated the taste but half an hour later I discovered Utopia. "Never mind the taste I will do that again".

I got married to a lass from just down the road in Edinburgh in 1973 and we had two children. I celebrated their arrival not with family and friends but with a bottle of booze. My Daughter, Jennifer is now 32, and a teacher and psychologist and beautiful person. She has red hair, but never call her Ginger! She has a son called Alistair, my Grandson, he is such a cute wee lad, full of fun, which is a great reflection on his Mother. I have a Son, Jonathan who is a chip off the old block and can't seem to settle into anything as far as a career is concerned. He is Addicted to any kind of liquid or substance which makes him feel better about himself. I love him dearly and pray for his recovery each day. He has a daughter, my only Granddaughter, and so lovely, she is ten at the time of writing. She is a beautiful girl with blond hair and blue eyes. Remarkable really as she is a quarter Jamaican. I am blessed because I was given sobriety. I can appreciate and am grateful for all the natural gifts in my life.

My wife, but now ex-wife as we divorced in 1993, and I started out in Edinburgh, my drinking was heavy but excused by all as I was the life and soul of many a party. Next, a geographic to London area where I worked for a Recording Company as a Promoter come salesman for the records and bands. This came about after working in a boring bank in Edinburgh and also playing guitar in a Rock Band. Rock and roll was more exciting, and I could excuse my drinking, so I resigned from the bank and went to the recording company for fame, fortune, drugs and alcohol.

Five years later I was in a mess and I decided, (Alcoholics should be banned from making decisions while active) that being my own boss was a good idea, much to the groans of my wife and family. I was always full of good intention and ideas, I just never carried them through to completion, but I did drag my family with me, poor souls!!

Geographical moves are a feature of me having good ideas, so eventually we arrived in the Scottish Borders.

Unfortunately every time we moved my head came with me.

By this time Alcohol consumption had turned me into a devious, manipulative, dishonest and cheating monster. I stole from my Wife, Children, Mother, Father and most of all from myself. I stole money, trust, love and self respect.

So, my wife eventually gave me the ultimatum. Change or bog off!! How rude is that!!

So I changed!!

I joined Alcoholics Anonymous and that is the only thing in my life that I had done up to that point that I have not regretted in some way. AA helped me remain sober with contentment and a growing self worth. The program changed me into a person that functioned as a human being. The one God always meant me to be in the first place. AA taught to be a reasonable, fair, polite and honest person. I asked AA people to sponsor me and help me with the program. This is a piece of humility for me as I don't like being told what to do. I listened and became teachable at last.

However I changed but my wife chose to remain the same, and two trains on different tracks usually end up at a different station especially if they are going in different directions.

You guessed it, when I was four years sober we got divorced, after 20 years of her as a hostage and me as a tramp living in a posh house. I felt crippled and empowered at the same time. I did not drink, this is a miracle.

At that time I met the present holder of the post 'Mrs B.' , we were married in 1994, discounting the odd flair up or two as we are both pretty fiery and I am still childlike in my behaviour at times.

We have a wee Daughter, Alisha. My wife, is a wonderful person who lives a day at a time without the AA program, truly remarkable.

When I got sober I went to college, after I got divorced, at the age of 43 and retrained as a Counsellor and studied Management of caring in business and finance.

MY mother died after 7 years of my sobriety. I did not drink, another miracle. I felt I made amends to her by behaving like the son she always wanted. She begged me to stop drinking for 20 years. When I got sober she often offered me a 'wee sherry' as I was 'ok' now. I would say 'no thank you' and leave it at that. I am learning compassion for the thoughts and feelings of others.

I worked in the law courts for four years helping Police witnesses to give evidence before studying to be a Paramedic with the Ambulance Service. I served as a Medic for five years and I thought I had finally found my vocation. I loved it and I was good at it. It was exciting and very worth while. My colleagues respected me and I respected myself (long awaited). However I was unlucky with the number of distressing types of jobs I was assigned to and developed Post Traumatic Stress Disorder, an often fatal illness quite akin to Alcoholism in its symptoms. An illness that results in addiction for many of its sufferers. I have not had a drink, another miracle. I relived all the episodes I thought I was coping with and collapsed in a heap one day unable to carry on. It happens to a lot of Paramedics but is kept fairly quiet as it is bad for recruitment. But I have not had a drink or drug since my sobriety date of 4th November 1989 at 4 pm.
So, here I am in Grand Canaria, in the sun, still recovering

from PTSD and a member of the Arguineguin International English Speaking meeting.

I am retired now through ill health, (PTSD), and my vocation now is to help people who still suffer from addiction. I love to see them get better although the percentages are very small for those that do recover, but if one makes it them my life is fulfilled.

Thank you all in the fellowship for my years of sobriety and service, especially those in the Borders of Scotland and the North East of England. Thanks for all you have given me,

written while in Gran Canaria

Forty Seven
Journey to France
by
Arthur and Marmite

HI, from rainy France I am in a wifi area, at McDonalds cordon blue, sending out emails for those that need to know.

I told Marmite we were going to France and that I would drive the car there after taking the Ferry from Las Palmas GC to Portimao Portugal.

Porti ' meow ' said marmite that sounds good to me. Will there be other pussies there? Meowed Marmite.

You never know our luck, I replied, I have never encountered a Portuguese pussy before!

The Ferry was on time, Spanish time, it was late. It also arrived with two big dents, one at the bow and one at the stern {Maritime ME hold me back} chill with the lingo.

Before I go any further I have a Spanish keyboard doing US English things, so the ? commas and ,,, question mark thingies are all mixed up(><. Och, forget it.

Onward with the journey. Successfully on board Maritime Marmite {MM} and I climbed the six floors, no lift available, it was busy with human creatures trying to fit too much, as usual, into the space provided. It won't go I heard one say. No it won't I whispered to MM cause it only takes four people, not four people and four cases! Da! So we climbed up the stairs, ladder or whatever it is on a boat!

Breathing as heavily as a fit 61 year old carrying suitcase, bag, camera, goody bag and a cat box, MM was quite exhausted when we reached the reception. Hola ,or whatever the

Portuguese equivalent is? I informed the young Chica
Guappa I have a cabin reserved. I felt sooo posh until she
looked at me and then the cat. In sickeningly perfect English
she informed me that animals go at the bottom of the ship in
the kennels, where you got on. Oh dear Posh fell through the
porthole. So all the way back down again to bowels of the
ship........and back up, poor me!
The cabin was fantastic with two single beds and shower
bathroom. Three picture windows, all 6ft x four ft. looking out
seaward to the direction of travel. I was at the Bows. So
excited..... until later . Good food in a pleasant restaurant and
reasonably priced. The ship has left the harbour and the sea is
calm for now but later, oh dear!
Wind, no gales, the sea rises and so does the boat at the front
{bows} especially. What goes up must come down. Crash,
thump and then the waves hit the side. Rolly, polly, let's be
sick. But being of seafaring stock on my Dads side I felt only a
wee bit odd for a while and then it went away. Phew!!
I met several interesting people. One, a German car dealer
from Tenerife. Two, a gay Englishman also from Tenerife with
two large.........Dogs. I know what you're thinking. Three, a gay
Englishman from GC. He was very camp, but quite amusing.
Gays boys are sailors obviously, and German car dealers and
Scottish adventurers.
Each night at eleven pm we were allowed to go and visit our
animals and also when we got into Funchal, Madeira. There
was a very large ocean liner in the port which we reckoned
must have housed 5000 sick travellers. Sick in the head, who
would choose to go up and down side to side rather than sit

on a beach or explore a country properly??? Can you imagine the video film being shown to the neighbours when they got home? We saw 25 ports and docks, and the same number of countries from a bus window, more up and down, side to side. Did you speak to anybody, NO, we learnt all about the country from an 18 year old tour guide. She would know a lot!!!!!!!!!!!

Back to the ship. Madeira is a beautiful looking island and I think a visit would be good. The passengers boarded for Porti meow. A circus came on board, big wagons and strange looking folk. Thinking about it I suppose they have to reproduce the humans to continue the circus so inbred in best. Keep it in house and all that!! Bad boy Arthur, very judgmental. That night we went down to the kennels and OMG Marmite had grown into a Tiger. A real one. No, sorry wrong cage. The circus had two lions, two tigers, and many other animals to boot. Marmite was terrified by the sounds of the other Cats and ate nothing that day. She has been very attentive ever since. I like that, she is my travelling buddy.

An hour or two on a ship is quite exhilarating for me, looking at the waves, the excitement of travel and especially when something new is on the horizon. In particular a new beginning. How many times have I done that now? Child to Adult life {didn't grow up, mature or have any sense, except party, party}. Then to leave home, get married, have children, move houses and geographically change environments.

Get sober, join AA, get divorced, and lose security, family and children. Meeting new people as a result of losing everything in a day's decision. What have I done? I grew up, that's what.

New partner, marriage, new friends, new career, sobriety without end and renewing relationships with my children. A personal relationship with a special person, then a child when I thought I had done all that before. I did well the second time round. Whoever gets anything right the first time?

Back to the journey, I am not very focused, never have been. Too many interesting things going on somewhere else in my brain. We docked in Porti meow at 11am on the Sunday morning. I was very enthusiastic to use my new navigation system in the car.

Guess what, 1 kilometre and I was lost, took the wrong turning. But I did see Porti meow and hope never to see it again. It is a dump. So is the ensuing coastline to Spain. Been there done that, MOVE ON.

Good roads, motorway all the way to Brittany. Taking 27 hours with many pee stops totalling 3 hours. So, 24 hours driving on cruise control. At the north end of Spain I came through the mountains and ski resorts which I did not know were there, I am so educated, not. I stopped for a bite to eat and when I came out there was an inch of snow on the ground. Blizzard time, so MM and I had a discussion on what to do so we picked the first snow plough and followed it through the mountain roads safely to the other side. Which is a bugger cause I wanted to see the area. All I saw was the rear end of the plough. Best laid plans and all that stuff. Got through and stopped for a while as my eyes were tired. Next day pouring rain so the planned camping was awash. Press on said MM. I blame the whole thing on the cat's decisions. But cats don't get lost do they, they are just where they are, and that's it really.

It is amazing how far one can push oneself when the end is nigh. I reach the end of the trail in Pontivy mid-afternoon on the Monday and booked into the hotel Rohan where we had stayed previously in October. The owners are a Gay couple and Jaqui remembered me from before. He also welcomed the Cat , MM, oh how sweet!!!

I love the rooms there and he gave me one with a bath, oh a bath, fantastic. The room was themed as the Jazz room with musical instruments all over the walls. Suited me down to the ground and very comfortable. I went out and treated myself to a meal at twenty euros. Three course and far too much but, brilliant cuisine and drink included. Off to bed for an early night. I let MM out of her box and she slept on my bed, what a bad boy.

Next morning an appointment with the estate agent Doug Seally, Englishman, and his French staff. All was well apart from a few hicks. No electricity, no water and the fosse septique needed up dating, but nothing I was not expecting. Got the keys and off to our new home.

No water or electricity since I moved in so it has been camping in the house for two weeks now although I did stay in the Motel at night with Kari and Alisha for four nights, which was a blessing as it was near freezing in the cottage. They are away home now and we have chosen the Kitchen, Bathroom, doors and tiles so far so my work is cut out for the next few weeks, or years more like. I love it here it is so

beautiful even in the winter, Hiver. French is coming on as you see!!!!!!!!
The electric came today so we are connected to the grid but only with the antiquated supply from cave man time! At least I have light and a wee bit power for the drill etc. any more and the fuse trips, Ho Hum another crazy day in paradise! Hopefully the water tomorrow.
Still no water………………………1st march demain.
Progress for now and freezing the nuts off, but Marmite keeps my feet warm. Missing everybody now they have gone. It is strange how I desire company while at the same time enjoy the isolation. This is part of the consequences of Post Traumatic Stress Disorder (PTSD). The desire to handle relationships and be with people, alongside the fear of my own reactions to situations with people, places, and things. It is not an ideal way to live but an illness is an illness carrying symptoms which have to be treated or accepted. There is no cure and that hits me hard sometimes especially as I have now two incurable diseases with regard to my Alcoholism and PTSD.
However I have the ability and courage to share my experiences and knowledge with others who suffer from the same conditions both in Alcoholics Anonymous and with my counselling clients.
Back to the French experience, now where was I in the cottage's jungle of refurbishment. Ah yes no water. Time for another visit to the water company, SAUR. After several kilometres and hours of searching the town of Loudiac I

eventually found the porta cabin used as an excuse for an office, tucked behind garages on the industrial estate.

I entered with fear and in trepidation of my French lingo abilities, only to find out I was quite right, my French was crap. But the lady behind the desk was charming and very helpful and I think we both enjoyed the sign language, diagrams and drawings to simulate a conversation. One might even have called it communication. The Bretons are great, charming and friendly if you only try a few phrases even if they might resemble a babbling Scotsman's attempt at cave man tactics. No, I did not grab her by the hair! Up to this point all of the contact with SAUR had been by telephone and through the estate agent. It had been frustrating to say the least, with various neighbours attempting to establish a water supply for me, but in desperation I finally plucked up the courage to go in person to the SAUR office. What the lady did or who she contacted I have no idea but I did make out the word 'demain' and something that resembled 'travalier' so I assumed that meant they were coming tomorrow and left with a big smile and a 'bonjournie', clever boy!

Tomorrow came and the time dragged by as it does when you are waiting for someone. Especially when I was anxious as to whether I had heard correctly, or not. I had been told by the estate agent that the water was not switched off, and by SAUR that the water was not disconnected.

The man from SAUR arrived, you have no idea the elation such a small event can cause when you are on your own and solely responsible for your attempts to sort the problem. Well the guy shook my hand as they all do, which is one of the more palatable traditions of the French in Brittany. He had a big smile and walked into the house, opened up the cupboard containing the water meter, disconnected it, took out the plug they had inserted to cut off the supply and connected the pipe back up. Bingo water on tap. The bastards should have known all along that it was capped off, but evidently nobody keeps a record of such an event. Oh well onward and upward. Electricity, Water and LPG for gas, to cook and heat one room.

Did I get the drill out, no I got the TV out of it's box to hook up the video and computer. Entertainment at night now with a hot meal, cups of tea, I was as happy as a pig in shit. Just the Telephone and internet to sort now, easy peasy. But I didn't know about the telephones in France, a monopoly of Orange or Orange. So the next day I went to the orange shop, oh dear!

Why Oh Dear? Well the French government are even inquiring about the suicide rate in the workforce of Orange. The pressures are evidently enormous for the staff and they are preferring to jump rather than endure. It was not a great surprise to me on my first visit to the Orange shop on Pontivy high street. The queues were ten deep and the store and it took over an hour of frustration to be served. John an old AA friend even took a seat and picnic table with him when his TV box blew up one stormy night. They didn't even blink in surprise, I think they may even have joined him in a cuppa from his flask! I diverse not for the first time. I did the deal and was to get Telephone, internet and TV in the same package. One week later it was all complete, so some things work ok.

And so to the next chapter, the grand building after the very satisfying demolition of a pretty grotty kitchen, garage and cow shed. The demolition derby.

LANRIVAUX, ST. CONNEC

Forty Eight
Demolition derby

Just give me a good reason to batter something with a sledge hammer and I am more than happy. The plan was set in my head. Keep at least three jobs on going at one time, inside and outside the house to give variety. I know how bored I get doing the same thing day in day out. Also to get the fresh air in my lungs as an alternative to the dust, muck and smells created by the refurbishment of an old property.
Now this was the perfect way to meet the neighbours. Not that the French are nosy! But we are in the country and it is only natural to understand that they would be curious about these new, incomers, from a different planet trashing part of their heritage. I was not aware however, that it is best to get agreement about your plans from the locals. Silly of me really, I should have realised that our affairs were the talk of the community and that they had a copy of the rules and regulations imprinted on their brains and, a direct telephone link to the local Mayor, who used to be the school teacher in St Connec, a mile up the road, for all of ten children. He was a VIP in local terms. However once the Mayor had visited our site there were few further problems. It was old Anthony at the back of us who had complained as I had decided to replace old existing windows at the back of the property. The frosty window was 60 centimetres too close to his garden so he objected and I had to put the frosted glass back in and take away the shiny new opening ones which made the back

look so much nicer. But not in his eyes evidently. Ho Hum, onward and backward.

I decided to keep a photographic record of before and after. I do tend to forget just how gradual changes can merge into one another leaving the past in a haze of progression. It would also create a record for future developments and details of pipe work for future generations of wee Biggsies. The first task was to knock a wall down between the garage and the number two bedroom hence creating a large living room downstairs. I had also measured up the entire building to a scale of one centimetre to one metre. The Kitchen also had walls to knock down, opening it up into a kitchen-diner. There were to be three bedrooms upstairs, with a mezzanine and shower room with toilet. Ambitious, as were many of the tasks I was to undertake. I had never before stretched my vast DIY skills, accumulated over 40 years of renovating houses on a minor scale, to such an awesome challenge. The loft space was massive and the plans were drawn up. This would be the biggest house Kari and Alisha had ever lived in to date. I had previously owned a large seven double bedroom mansion in the town of Wooler in Northumberland, it was also haunted but that is a story in itself involving my son and daughter Jonathan and Jennifer, when they were little children. I diverse........again.

I suppose on reflection part of my motivation for the project in hand was to provide a place for the whole family to be together at some stage. Children and grandchildren and a happy Grandpa Biggs. There was a time when I could not have envisaged such a union through my alcoholic haze.

Gratitude is hard work, but a joyful experience. But don't get too excited, there was disaster afoot. My visions were shattered sooner than I could ever expect.

Meanwhile, to develop the project in a sustainable manner I would have to obtain the assistance of some professionals. In other words ask for help!! Not easy for a grandiose Alcoholic, but needs must prevail.

I needed a new Fosse tank and the electrical system required a wee upgrade. All the wiring and plugs and sockets must go and be replaced with a complete new system which adhered to the French regulations. I contacted the selling agent, Doug, who put me in touch with Mr. Know it all, which is quite common for electricians in my experience. Don't know why, they just are!

He was English speaking from the Channel Island of Jersey. Very good at his job and meticulous to the degree where I was tearing out my hair with frustration as he nosed around all the jobs I was doing, suggesting and pointing out better ways of doing everything, Agh!

The guy who put in our Fosse tank and new main drains was also English but altogether a different character. Friendly, and he also played Guitar. Anyone who plays a musical instrument seems to have more about them in a rounded sort of way. Just in my opinion of course!

This whole process, even though there were plans drawn and permissions required from the local Mayors Office, tended to develop on a day to day basis. Meeting problems head on and adjusting plans accordingly. Right up my street, it is so much more exciting that way. Thank God I am not a Mr. Percentage, there was never panic, just a search for a solution, very Alcoholics Anonymous and another application of the principals of the twelve step program.

THE LOFT SPACE.
 The roof was an A frame, tiled on top of wooden boards and solid as a rock. Literally, as I was soon to find out, when it came to driving nails into the three hundred year old beams. This posed a problem, overcome by drilling and screwing, but not before a succession of bent nails, mini sledgehammers, broken fingernails and language of which the southern Irish would have been proud. ''Feckin royt dey wood''.
Woodworm, not a little, but a lot, mostly old holes but it was difficult to tell with some so I sprayed the whole place up and down, twice. Word of advice, wear a mask, I was ill for week after the application, and probably did lasting damage to my wellbeing for ever more, who knows, but that is just me, wham bam and get it done! If I had worms before, I didn't now!
Marmite, remember, my cat, was a clever girl, she hid in the bedroom under my duvet while I sprayed and banged above her in the loft space. Just as well really, as she may have sacrificed one or two of her nine lives already.

THAT FIRST SWING OF THE SLEDGEHAMMER.
Oh my, what courage in took each time an old wall needed the ''Rambo'' treatment. The debate that went on in my head 'what if', but then, one just has to do it, take aim, deep breath, close eyes and swing..................Oops, no turning back

now. French walls are made of very large, thin, hollow, ceramic tile things. Very tough, sturdy structures but when you wallop them with the trusty, Big Bertha, they just crumble into dust heaps on the floor. I must have shifted dozens of tons of the stuff from the house to the old cow shed outside in the garden. That was it though, and as time drifted by I became more courageous and extremely dangerous, mostly toward myself and of course Marmite. Now Marmite had evolved from 'Maritime Marmite' to " the Elusive Companion". I would see her at night around seven o'clock', she would sleep on my bed or disappear into the night darkness and reappear with the odd live mouse. Which we would then spend the next hour chasing around the kitchen, much to her delight, but neither to the mouse's or mine.

In the morning she would disappear again as soon as I picked up any sort of implement or tool for the days demolition rota. I found later that she spent the whole day under the floor boards up in the loft. That is until the Electrician turned up to prepare for the new wiring. He was one unpopular cookie with Marmite. Actually he never saw the cat. As soon as he pulled up in his van outside she disappeared. Can you imagine being Marmite in her cosy wee hideaway and suddenly being pursued by a giant whirly, spinning wheel with massive teeth, threatening your very precious tail with severance! The sound itself must have been terrifying. Poor wee Marmite.

The house was now ready to be rebuilt, step by step from the bottom up. Whenever Karen came across to be with me in France we went out to all the DIY shops and ordered the tiles, bathroom furniture, and kitchen. I wasn't all in favour of the choices as they were always top of the range and cost a mini fortune. I always felt that Karen's heart was never in France which proved to be the case in the near future, especially after Alisha proved her hatred for all things French including the school and education system.

However I got on with the project each time they returned to England where they were until the house was complete.

The only job I did not undertake was the electrics and also the installation of the Kitchen. Everything else was down to me and my accumulation of DIY skills from all of the 30 plus houses I had lived in over the past 40 years.

I laid the tiles on the floor. All 230 square meters of them, plus the wall tiles in the bathroom and kitchen and shower room and painted all the doors, ceilings and walls.

I converted the upper storey from a loft space into three bedrooms, a shower room and a mezzanine. It was all my own design and was passed by the fussy French Mayor and planning department.

I put in five new windows, French widows and three Velux windows in the roof, plus replacing all the plumbing in the house.

All to no avail because when Alisha and Karen came to join me in France we only lasted two months before Karen wanted to run away to the Middle East.

I never complained but inside I was devastated to leave my creative project. I was very proud of my efforts and felt they were never appreciated.

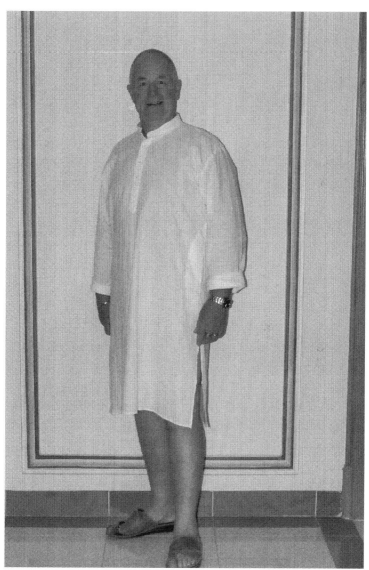

2012 living in Muscat, like a local.

Forty Nine
Move to the Middle East

With the French experience now behind us, and considering Alisha's schooling, it was time to take stock again as the employment prospects for Karen in France were poor to say the least. Hence the inevitable, Karen stuck with her head in the computer for hours on end searching for the new adventure.

There were quite a number of options that reared their heads, but most notably, the Middle East. There was also the offer of a head of department in the old school in the North East but that did not seem to offer the challenge Karen needed before settling the Gypsy within.

The money angle was an important one as we had accrued a sizable debt through the move from Gran Canaria and the refurbishment of the house in France. However, there were other considerations. The challenge of something new, which has always been an issue with both of us as we get bored very quickly if there is not enough stimulus within the present situation. Also the fact that we were not yet ready to settle back in the UK, or France for that matter.

There were many options with regard to jobs abroad but the ones that hit the spot seemed to those in Arabia. We had never experienced that part of the world or the culture of Muslim people in there own environment. Visits to these places give one a false impression of the reality of living in that environment. The changes in seasons, or more appropriately the lack of seasons at all, is something my head cannot accept for any length of time as I have found out from our experiences.

So, to cut a long bedraggled story short, Karen found a job in Muscat, Oman in a school called the United Private School. It turned out to be slightly different from our expectations, as I will elaborate in as nice a manner as possible.

I shall first describe our arrival in the middle of the night after a very pleasant flight with Qatar Airways. One's own TV, free food and drink and very amenable care by the flight attendants. Ok good start, off to a flier. The new head teacher, Mr Chris, met us at the airport. Everybody bets called Mister in front of his or her first name, which after a while is very annoying, as my culture does not recognise Mister without the last name present. Where did they get that idea?

Observation number one. It is a scary experience away from your own familiar surroundings. Lack of knowledge can be exhilarating or frightening according to your level of awareness. We were tired from the journey and acceptance is the best policy until rational judgements can be accessed. The apartment seemed huge, with two bedrooms, living room, kitchen, dining area and two bathrooms with baths. Couldn't be better.

In the following few days we were introduced to several members of staff, mostly management, and wined and dined by the director Mr Nigel. A very large character, with a wide girth and a soft-spoken BBC accent. If BBC has an accent as it is gradually infiltrated by regionalisation. There was Miss

Wendy from South Africa who responded well to my flirtations, so she was a conquest in the 'on my side kind of way'. Miss Wendy's friend Miss Jackie who taught English at Alisha's prospective new school.

Mr Nigel had a 'boy', who had a wife, who lived in house with Mr Nigel, on a permanent basis. He was called 'Shanto' and his wife, 'lisa'. He was the bosses 'Chunky Walla', more on that in a moment. What did he do for Mr Nigel, well er......everything!, and that I think, speaks for itself, the rest is up to your imagination, pure and simple, or not so pure and simple. Shanto was from Sri Lanka, and had lived and attended to Mr Nigel's needs for several years. It really was a sick relationship and definitely exploitation by the upper classes over the poor.

It is fair to say however, we were settling in to a very elegant life style, in what looked like a very attractive place, that is, until the sun came up as we were to learn over the next few months. Initial impressions are important but there is the 'rose tinted glasses' effect and the romantic rush of a brand new start, although we should have learned from the Gran Canaria experience. Old dogs, new tricks and all that!!!

Karen was soon to start work at her new school and Alisha would be introduced to her new classmates at the United Private School of Muscat. I was there for a month to settle them in and help iron out any bumps on the way. They were at different sites so it was as if they were at different schools, which is always best for the student in that circumstance. Alisha was 'buddied up' with several girls in her year eight class. They were of various nationalities, Arabic, Turkish,

Indonesian, etc. This would be a very wide and varied experience for Alisha, which would hold her in good stead for her future.

I was summoned to the boss's office when we settled in to be interviewed for the position of Operations Manager for three of the five schools attached to the group. The job spec. detailed the management of the security, domestic and maintenance supporting the teachers in their daily duties. The job itself was easy but the heat made it very difficult to function as it topped 40 degrees most days. The schools ran on a very disciplined regime. These children had Grandparents who had never been to school and parents who had been catapulted into the modern world by the presence of oil under their feet. They were mostly millionaires now and they enjoyed a standard of living which many a western peasant would have envied, including me.

Their background was based on a tribal culture with a Sheik at the top as the leader who would be respected by all of the tribe. The women were kept in their place and were just beginning to assert their rights as a human being but still played second fiddle to the men. Restaurants were men only as were the mosques but they had rooms at the back for families to eat and pray.

It seemed very strange at first to enter the shopping malls where the men all wore Dish Dashes, long over pyjamas like Wee Willie Winky. Minus the candle of course but they did have a funny wee hat called a Kumar, a bit like an up turned flower pot with fancy designs on the side.

The women wore Abaja dresses and Hijabs to cover their heads and in some cases their faces, but all of them had super duper designer clothes and shoes underneath. I have to say I could not see the point of it all unless it was to protect them from the heat, but the Abajas were almost all black, so that did not seem to make any sense to me! Unless it was in the event they got run over by a bus or something!

The shopping malls were always very busy as they were the only place with air conditioning and in the daily heat that was a welcome relief, so we joined them all after school for oodles of Costa coffees.

After a month or two of the high life, being entertained by our new employers, things started to settle down when I returned to join them after visiting France.

I started the new job in earnest getting used to the heat of the day. I had an air con office but most of my work required me to visit different parts of the schools.

I befriended the IT manager called David who was a native of South Africa. He was coloured which meant that one of his parents was white, and one black. Life had not been easy for him in his home country and his Father had been targeted and shot for having a white wife.

One morning I arrived at the school in our hire car. A police car drew up beside me and an official looking Officer approached me. He was wearing a uniform which indicated that he held a high rank in the force. These guys were not to be messed with and ex pats did as the authorities wanted or you were deported without question or argument.

He asked me who I was, and what job I did at the school. I told him I was the new Operations Manager, my wife also worked at the school as a teacher and Alisha attended as a student.

He asked questions about where my car came from and how much I paid for it. I told him the cost and he looked at me and then back at his car and astonished me by asking me if I would like to rent his top of the range VW Passat CC for half the price of the hire car. He also said I would be protected from prosecution if anything went wrong, like an accident or speeding fine.

I could not believe my luck and did not realise this was a done deal before he even spoke. Visitors who work in the Arab State of Oman are well advised to people please the authorities, especially when they offer a brilliant deal with guaranteed protection!

Needless to say we were now in proud possession of a fabulous car.

He turned out to be chief of police for forensic operations and lived in a fantastic house with a swimming pool in the middle of it. We were entertained in his home and met his wife and children on several occasions. His children attended to the school where we worked.

To work in Oman we had to become resident which was a process carried out at the police station where we gave our finger prints and details to the authorities to receive a 3 year resident visa for working in Muscat.

The country is fascinating but very dry and arid but when it rained the place instantly flooded as the design of the roads left out a vital part of engineering, there were not drains, so the water ran like rivers flooding the streets and sometimes killing unfortunate people who were caught out in the open. Oman is not somewhere I would return to but the people I met there through the fellowship of AA were wonderful and I still keep in touch with them through social media.

I attended two AA meetings a week in the centre of Muscat which had been set up by ex-pat workers but the membership consisted of seventy per cent Muslim boys and men who had fallen foul of western influences.

If any men had a problem with Alcohol, which of course is totally against their religious teachings, they must present themselves at the Police station where they are referred to the rehab hospital in Saudi Arabia. They are allowed to stay there free of charge for up to a year after which they return to their own country.

They are put through the 12 step program at the hospital but their problems after they return to their homeland are complicated as their families do not want to know them as they have disgraced the Muslim and Tribal culture.

As had been usual in all the other places we had been, Karen became discontent when things did not go her way. Even though she was promised promotion, we still did a runner back to the UK under a blanket of resentment created by her discontent.

So we went back to the UK with the intention of settling in Hexham.

I should have known that would not last but I put every effort into making it work for Alisha and the sake of our marriage.

LETTER FROM OMAN to AA in the UK

For 25 years my Addiction developed from the first drink at the age of fourteen, which I thought was a social drink, to near death experiences and total destruction of my life. It also attacked all those with whom I came into contact, especially my Family and friends. Addiction is the worst 'Illness' I know. I read once that if Addiction had a voice it would surely read like this:

'My name is Addiction and I am a disease. I hate meetings and Higher Powers. I hate anyone who has a Program. All who come into contact with me and practice my principals of dishonesty, deviousness, manipulation, greed and resentments I promise them death and suffering. I am cunning, baffling, powerful and patient. I have killed millions and I love it.'

It caught me with the element of surprise. It pretended to be my friend. It gave me false comfort. It was there when I was lonely and brought feelings of self destruction. It made me hurt. It made me cry. Worse yet, it made me so numb I could neither hurt nor cry. I couldn't feel anything at all. This was true pain and suffering.

I thought it gave me instant gratification and all I got was long term suffering. It was always there. When things were going right or wrong in my life, I invited it in. Addiction destroyed all good things in my life.

People don't take addiction seriously. They take strokes seriously, heart attacks, even diabetes they take seriously. All of these are also consequences of Addiction. I hate disease. Insanity replaces reality and peace.

But there is a solution; Addiction hates the Twelve Step Program, Meetings and Higher Powers. All weaken its resolve and it can't function properly.

However it is cunning baffling and powerful as it lies dormant waiting quietly and patiently. You don't see it but it can grow, through resentments, dishonesty and devious behaviour and reappears bigger than ever.

It only exists when you exist. But it is always there. There is no cure

Once an Addict, always an Addict. It is the only illness that tells you don't have it. The illness of denial. I experienced exactly this as a practicing Alcoholic. So what has AA given me more than just stopping drinking?

Courage to change the things I can, that's what!

In contrast, 22 years on from those 25 years of degradation I have retired from serving as a Paramedic Advance Technician, working on Accident & Emergency front line Ambulances in the North of England.

Before joining the Ambulance Service I had a wide variety of experience in my life's journey after I found Sobriety in 1989. In 1993, I was trained to support Victims of crime from the effects of rape and sexual assault on male and female victims to Families of Murder Victims. I studied and qualified as a Counsellor. I was then asked to establish a new service providing support and protection for Police and Civilian witnesses in the Courts in the North East of England.

In 1997 I formed a team of counsellors in Northumberland, UK, providing care and counselling for clients with acute Drug and Alcohol addictions, offering help to both the user and the family. I also gave talks to schools on the effects of Alcohol on the individual and the Family consequences thereafter.

During this time I rekindled an old interest and qualified as a Black Belt Instructor with the Karate Union of Great Britain. This was one of many examples throughout my Sobriety of dreams turning into reality.

Today, I don't have destructive relationships and have been blessed with a wonderful family, along with a multitude of true friends.

I moved to Gran Canaria with my Wife and Daughter in August 2006. I worked there voluntarily as a therapist, practising Counselling and Reflexology. All these things happened for me when I found sobriety in AA. They can happen for you too.

My family and I lived there for Five years, where I attended the meetings of Arguineguin, San Fernando and Playa del Ingles. My thanks go to all the AA members who supported and befriended me on those islands in the middle of the Atlantic Ocean.

I am now a member of the Arab states intergroup through my home group in Muscat, Oman. We moved here after a brief episode in Brittany, France. France was like an AA graveyard, but there are some very good AA members keeping the meetings open despite massive geographical difficulties due to the size of the country. I still will return there and if any AA people visit the area then please try to make a special effort to support the resident sober community.

I celebrated, with God's grace and membership of Alcoholics Anonymous, being clean and sober for 8036 consecutive days on the 5th November 2011. I did this with my new found Omani, Egyptian and American AA friends in Muscat.

I have experienced the positive effects of recovery through coping with divorce, bereavement and trauma. I have witnessed the destructive effects of this 'illness' on a member of my own Family but more importantly, I have seen the positive results of recovery from potentially hopeless situations. There is a 12 Step programme on offer, enabling individuals to find hope and self worth when they imagine all is lost. This is a devastating and progressive illness, and on many occasions, fatal.

I hope that others who suffer from addiction can benefit from my recovery and also access the 12 step solution to this physical, mental and spiritual illness.

Why has my life turned around? Because I became willing to change and I don't drink or take mind altering substances any more, one day at a time. Yesterday is gone and tomorrow is a vision of hope which just leaves today to live the best I can as a <u>reasonable, fair, polite, honest and compassionate human being</u>.

I have never regretted joining AA. I have only ever experienced the effects of the 12 Promises since letting go and letting God, and accepting help in the fellowship. The

members own selfless sharing and support is so powerful.
They are all wonderful people,

Love in Fellowship to all, Arthur, 3769 Way, Muscat, Oman.

Fifty
2013 = THE BEGINNING OF ANOTHER END

I had planned to go to France to finish the refurbishment of the Longere as a final purge to see if we could sell it. I have done many things in my marriage with which I have not been entirely comfortable and this was definitely one of them.
I had spent at least a year on my own in that house while Karen got on with her own agenda. I should have seen the writing on the wall but whoever said 'love is blind' was a very perceptive person.
Karen and I had fallen out the evening before I was to leave to travel to catch the ferry in Portsmouth. I had been doing some research on the internet about lesbianism, both for counselling and personal reasons, Karen had been flirting with a lesbian relationship with her best friend.
Unfortunately when you 'google' lesbian, it Cookies onto all sorts of pornographic literature and content. A pop-up appeared of a nude woman with her legs spread so I closed it down or so I thought. So beware all who read this it can innocently ruin your marriage and give you heartache.
From that moment on Karen was intent on finishing our relationship, and the lady was not for turning as Maggie Thatcher once said, I knew I disliked that woman the first time I saw her on telly Thatcher not Karen! Then it turns out I was married to one and the same.
However I travelled on to France, exchanging texts with this individual who could no longer be called my partner but now, my adversary. I spent several days finishing the Longere project of which I was and still to this day, very proud. I could have done so much more but I spent a lot of time trying to

come to terms with the prospect of having lost my wife and much more importantly lost my Daughter.

Life is a very lonely planet when your relationship and soul mate leave you. It makes for a very deep whole to fill and at this time I felt the task was all too much for me to handle. Alone in France with no English speakers or telephone or mobile signal or internet. I planned suicide by Vagal Inhibition. I even decided the place, time and burning the house down around me. If it had not been for the faces and voices of my children that entered my head I would not be here today to write this confessional. I pray that my God will forgive me for these actions and thoughts as I know he does because I believe it was his intervention that stopped me that night. I had received texts from my Daughter Jenifer, my Son Jonathan and my Sister Hilary to say they were sorry to hear my bad news and that they loved me and offered their support. I cried so many tears that week as I was continually over whelmed by grief.

I contacted my sister and arranged to travel back early on the ferry in order to stay with her for a couple of nights to get my head together. Another of God's plans came into being as I travelled back. There was a storm of the magnitude I had not experienced before. The waves were hitting the front of this enormous ferry and going over the top of the boat. Children were screaming, and the whole passenger list was heaving up in the toilets. There were only a handful of us left and we sat at the side to avoid the constant procession of vomiting souls heading for the first thing they could find to deposit their stomach contents. This was all a great distraction from my poor me predicament.

I had with me the contents of the Longere in a hired van which was to be an insight into my homecoming as I will convey shortly. The wicked witch of the North was not finished with me yet, there were more and shocking events to come in the next few days. Beware of a woman like Karen who has not even been scorned.

While in Windsor I went to the bank to withdraw a little cash to fill up the van to get home only to find Karen had stopped the joint account and I was officially penniless. I had to borrow from my big Sister to fill the tank and return to the North.

It was a long and very angry journey home, mixed with the grief, and remorse of my situation. I arrived in Northumberland, at our rented accommodation to find it empty, completely empty save a few broken pieces of furniture and some air looms from my side of the family. No knifes or forks, no linen or food, just an empty house where once my family had been.

Why? I have my theories but they are just that, theories. Built on evidence and some facts which I have explored on more than one occasion. If it had not been for my family, my friends in the fellowship and God's intervention, I would not have survived. That is not a theory that is a fact.

On reflection, the reasons for Karen's actions are fairly clear. She had planned this for some time, waiting for the right moment where she could divert her responsibility for her decisions to a third-party and I was the obvious choice. Nothing had been right since our joint return from our adventures. We were living in direct reach of her mother who has always been waiting for an opportunity to destroy our marriage. When Karen and I were away we were a couple with the most beautiful daughter anyone could dream of having and a good relationship.

Karen is also a person who needs constant stimulation. If she is not shocking others with her behaviour then she becomes restless. This has been a constant throughout our marriage and will always be there for Karen. On the other hand, I like stability, and I only put up with her actions because I loved her so much. Love is definitely blind.

Considering the efficiency and speed with which all this had been done, I am convinced, as countless others have pointed out, that this was pre-planned and as such very ruthless.

She had not at any stage considered the feelings or wellbeing of Alisha. For that I am both disappointed and angry. I can only pray that Alisha comes through all of this with a balanced mind and attitude towards the male sex and does not learn that this kind of behaviour is in any way acceptable towards another human being.

So what now? I had her instructions that this was to be amicable for the sake of Alisha. Emotional blackmail at its best. I was not to contact her, unless through her lawyer and he was an incredible bastard. Everything was to be shared fairly. That is a very open statement I was to learn to my cost, as Karen's fair does not relate to anything a reasonable human would understand. Karen's favourite attitude is 'my way or the highway' not just with me, but with every partner she has had in her life. She must be the most selfish person I have ever had the misfortune to fall in love with.

Well she is gone out of my life now. I am fortunate to have shared some wonderful experiences with her and many years of a one-sided relationship. My fault not hers, I let her do it, so be warned reader, a relationship is about loving and giving. She used to call me selfish, but there is a thing called 'mirroring' in counselling. This relates to a person reflecting their own problems onto another in order to justify their deviant behaviour. After a period of seven months of putting the pieces of my life's jigsaw back together, I have come out a wiser and stronger person. I have also found God in my life and wish to commit myself to the betterment of mankind. Will I ever find another partner? I don't know but I will be very careful with my next choice, or the next invitation. I do not want to be so badly treated or hurt so much again. The only constant in my life is the grace God and Jesus Christ, who suffered for my sins, but was resurrected as I am reborn to a better life.

On the 24th November 2013 I was confirmed as a Senior Soldier in the Salvation Army and this was my testament.

It feels like I have been on a long and torrid journey. But for 25 years – the only spirit i knew was at the bottom of a bottle of alcohol.

I demanded god's intervention but god was not listening --- or so i thought!!!!!!!

My life was unmanageable and no human power could relieve my alcoholism. Not doctors, psychiatrists, or clergymen.

I was alone, or so I thought!!!!!!!!!!!!!!!!!! —

I died once from the illness – but god was having none of it – he refused to let me go!

then one day after 15 years of deprivation and pain, especially for all around me who had begged me to stop - i had a spiritual experience which I can only put down to a god given moment.

4 friends approached me and told me they were tired of my behaviour, but they did it with kindness and care. I was confronted with a dilemma for which there was only one answer. I had to surrender, give up, let go of this insanity. I poured my vodka over the ground and from that moment I felt different. Something inside me had changed. I believe I was then in the hands of god.

I read a passage from the bible which makes a lot of sense to me now. It was about the paralysed man and his four friends who place him at the feet of Jesus. Pick up your bed and walk was the message. It was then that I realised that god could and would do for me what I could not do for myself.

I began to change from being devious, manipulative and dishonest to fair reasonable polite and honest, all brought about by a spiritual program. The 12 steps of alcoholics anonymous which has led me to standing here this morning.

I began to cherish each day and form honest loving and caring relationships. The St Francis prayer sums it up more succinctly. I believe I have learned compassion and how my experience can benefit others.

My god given AA sponsor bill once said to me there is only one thing you need to change Arthur --- everything. I'm a work in progress.

However, sometimes there is only one set of footprints in the sand as god carries me through times in my life when the pain is just too great.

I love my god as I love my two daughters, my son and my grandchildren. I have a life beyond my wildest dreams and that is why I am standing here in this uniform as a symbol of my gratitude. I see it as my act of faith and a proud moment.

Finally, when I walked in the doors of this building six months ago I was shown unconditional acceptance, love and understanding and that is why I wanted to come back and be a part of this wonderful fellowship. I am humbly asking god now to use me as a channel and instrument of his grace and peace to go out from here to do his will not mine.

Without the pain and deprivation - without the god given 12 steps of AA - without the love of the fellowships I would not have found salvation. - Without the love of god and my family and friends I would not be here today.

So thanks to God for choosing me to be a soldier in the Salvation Army.

ANOTHER NEW LIFE

CHAPTER ONE

I am writing again, starting in early December 2013, nine months after Karen walked out on our marriage. These months have been very difficult for me and I imagine also for Alisha.

I have ridden an emotional rollercoaster with thoughts of self-termination. I planned suicide by hanging from the banisters in the French property whilst burning the house down with the paraffin heater. Later when I returned to the North East, the memories of what was, both in my marriage and the ambulance service, I stood at the railway crossing searching for the courage to utilise a 125 express train on the Widdrington stretch of the East Coast line. The intensity of these feelings was a new low for me and I thought I had been to my rock bottom before while drinking. But this was entirely different as I was sober and aware of all the emotions. I think my saving grace at the crossing may have been compassion for the driver of the train and his family. It certainly had little to do with lack of courage on my part. I was ready to end it all.

Imagine a sixty five year old man left isolated from his family with no hope of being reunited. No thoughts of compassion from a wife to whom I felt I had given my life and soul. I certainly gave up my closeness to my family and many of my passions in the sporting world, such as tennis and golf.

I felt like a Jenga pile of wood pieces, knocked over because the opponent was not winning before completion of the game. This left only a decision to rebuild and start from scratch or abandoning the game altogether, there was no contest in that decision, the game was over.

I came to the realisation that if I focused on the negative aspects of my life at this time then I would feel no fulfilment, spiritually or mentally.

While in this state of mind it gave me a chance to re-evaluate my priorities. The wellbeing of my wife, Karen, would now be dropped to the bottom of the list and Alisha would be raised to the top, along with the rest of my family. Self pity would have to take a back seat. Thinking of the wellbeing of significant others in circumstances such as these is the only truly spiritual path.

Alisha will always be a treasured and positive part of my life. However she now resided with her Mother which in truth gave me cause for concern. Not because Karen is a bad mother but because she is quite unstable from time to time while suffering from her Rheumatic fever illness. This was a condition caused by Scarlet Fever in the early years of our marriage which accentuated her already bazaar behaviour contracted from an eccentric gene within her family. Her Grandfather had it and so did her Mother, they would have random aggressive outbursts which made no sense at all.

I think they are all spiritually dishonest people with no sense of compassion for anyone but themselves.

The spiritual nature of my own recovery from traumatic events in my life comes from a belief in a Higher Power. I believe there is no denying the power of the creation of the universe right through to the tiniest spiritual or material speck.

Since my calling to enter the Hall of the Salvation Army in Bedlington, I have felt the development of a journey to believe and trust in the will of God and I have chosen the Christian channel to access the source of that power greater than myself.

On entering the world of the Salvationists I have studied their Doctrines in conjunction with the scriptures of the Gospels and found them to be the best way to conduct the rest of my life under the guidance of God.

I am at last ready to have God remove my defects of character which in turn is allowing me access to my own true self.

I am stepping out of defensive mode today and will follow the teachings of Jesus and also wise humans such as Deepak Chopra.

On the 24th of November 2013 I was enrolled as a soldier in the Salvation Army corps in Bedlington. It was an emotional transition from the realm of the material to the spiritual.

Even though all my priorities have changed I still feel a deep sense of love for both my wives and all of the other women with whom I have been privileged to have close personal relationships.

I know I will always carry these loves in my soul, every person who has touched my heart still lives within my soul.

Karen's decision to adopt a two year separation, which I see as a process to achieve easy divorce for the faint hearted, caused me an immense amount of emotional grief.

I received letters from her solicitor, which contained content designed to hurt and demoralise me.

On a weekly basis I received letters from David Auld, her weasel solicitor, who dishes out punishment to people he has never met in order to satiate his own inadequacies, which impacted upon my spiritual wellbeing but only briefly. They contained content designed to cause the most injury to put me on the back foot.

However I have been through this before and know that solicitor's communication is constitutionally dishonest, deceitful and lacking in any moral fibre. Therefore I treated it with the contempt it deserved, well most of it anyway.

People told me not to worry as it was only the lawyer's intent on prolonging the process to make more money, which is probably true as they are all in my experience with the justice system, very dishonest. But there always has to be an instruction behind the action and for that, Karen is entirely responsible.

In the end she took out divorce proceedings and the courts dealt with the issue with complete insensitivity which actually matched Karen's attitude to every other human in general.

I believe in Karma and for Karen's actions she may be eternally doomed. No comment!!!!

Heartless? That is how it seemed at that moment in time, but that was to change in the coming months.

So the return from our adventures in foreign countries began
with a few wrong turns and ended in disaster as far as our
marriage was concerned. Mostly I felt the pain of Alisha's
anguish as she was an innocent bystander in the selfishness
of her Mother's decision.

On my part I am entirely satisfied with my behaviour
throughout the divorce proceedings and kept as close to
Alisha as possible despite the circumstances.

It has remained that way to this day and I think that Alisha
and I are as close as we ever were.

We see each other every Sunday after I have attended the
Salvation Army meeting and have some lunch together,
catching up on our weekly experiences and various
encounters with the big wide world. She has grown into a
very lovely woman both inside and out. She has also coped
really well with the change and sees the whole situation in a
positive light.

In truth we probably see each other more because we live
apart and when we do connect we have a very positive
relationship. Bonus all around, as I no longer have to listen to
Karen about her job day in day out. Cruel but true, as I am a
people pleaser with a desire to solve the anxieties of others.
This is a very exhausting pass time as I have found to my own
personal cost emotionally. The first line of the serenity prayer
covers this by saying "accept the things we cannot change".
When will I ever learn!!

On my part I have very many blessings to count. I have the
fellowship of Alcoholics Anonymous, the Salvation Army and

a new interest in music, lawn green bowls and too many other things to recount.

There is of course the most precious of my blessings and that is a very close and loving relationship with my children, grandchildren and all of the barmy army on my Sister, Hilary's side of the family.

It is only now I realise how big a wedge Karen had put between me and my family. I do not blame her as I am responsible for all my own thoughts and actions. I am just sorry I did not have the courage to follow my instincts and to be honest with Karen about how I felt. There is also Poppy my puppy who is fast becoming a "confident" in that I tell her everything in the hope she never learns to speak "human" speak!!

I think this is an appropriate time to stop the reflections and move on to how it is today. So onto the next chapter.

Poppy the Puppy

CHAPTER TWO

CLINICAL HYPNOTHERAPY - MOVING ON

I have always been fascinated by the prospect of being hypnotised, while at the same time quite scared of the prospect. I think because I like to be in control of myself and felt that hypnosis would take that away from me and leave me out control.

I entered the therapy sessions with a little trepidation, but also with an enthusiasm that I might encompass the prospect of changing the fearful existence caused by the numerous traumas in my life to date.

My Therapist of choice was an AA friend whom I had known for at least twelve years. She displayed a very caring and lively personality, with a deep spiritual nature, and I respected her recovery from her own demons.

Angela, my therapist took me back to my childhood memories and asked me to view them in a non-threatening way and asked me to try and respect my decisions and actions.

I cannot explain fully the process but I benefitted from the experience and learned some new processes to follow in order to find my own self-respect and wellbeing.

I feel more self aware do not look back with regret on my informative years giving power to those who hurt me or controlled me through my own fears.

So today I still drive taxis to earn a little more even though I am now sixty five with four pensions including the national pension. However I intend to retire next year and bother my family with regular visits, especially ones I have not seen for many years in Scotland, France and anywhere else I can find them.

I have a wee car now of my own, a Suzuki Alto sz4 and a wee puppy called Poppy, a Jack Russell terrier, who means the world to me as Jennifer my daughter, bullied me into getting her to keep me company, which she does, night and day as she sleeps at my feet under the covers of my bed.

I swore I would never let an animal in my bed and that lasted all of two nights as Jack Russell dogs are notoriously loyal and very determined.

So now for the first time in many years I am becoming fairly settled, although there is still a burning desire inside me to take off on another adventure.

I have thought about going back to the Canary Islands on many occasions as I still have very good and loyal friends that still live there with a simple and uncomplicated lifestyle. I am sure I would be happy for a while but become bored after a period of time, although the Salvation Army do a fantastic job there with the homeless and destitute.

 Still I have the burning passion within.

I have thought also about relocating to the North West of Scotland but there too I would need a purpose and I do not think there are a lot of options in that part of the world.

If I listen to my sensible self, which is not very often even now at my tender age, I will be staying at the wee pensioners cottage in Widdrington and use it as a base to go on my wanderings after I have retired myself from the taxi driving.

The people who live around me in my bungalow are very quiet and pleasant old blokes. The one next door, called Peter George is a very good Lawn Green Bowler and has introduced me to the game.

I love the competition and fresh air, also the peaceful nature of the game. I bought myself a set on bowls from a guy who is now too disabled to play and I found I am quite good at it, consequently I now have a place on the team each Saturday, so that is something to look forward to at the end of each week.

I realise some people live their lives in a straight line with minor adversities which seem to trouble them greatly.

I on the other hand seem to have become hardened through my experiences of personal and witnessed trauma to the extent that I do not fear death nor find the passing of others as any great problem. The only sadness I feel is if anyone younger than me dies and has not had the chance to make their way through life and experience the joys and knocks which make us who we are today.

Nor can I understand the persistent mourning of the living for the fortunate who have passed on to the next phase in their journey.

I hate the way we British seem to mourn rather than celebrate a life. If there is one thing I would like to change it is the present system of burial and cremation. Let's have a party and look forward to a life beyond our meagre physical existence. It cannot be any more warped than the life here on Earth, where the material becomes the priority and dishonesty and greed continue to destroy our spiritual wellbeing.

However, loneliness is a bitch and it cuts into my serenity. Poppy the Puppy has been a temporary solution but I miss just having someone around me that cares about me. I suppose I miss Karen's company despite the way she discarded me like a trophy no longer needed because it was gathering dust.

I had the feeling Karen felt the same way about the loneliness from things that Alisha said to me when we went out for Sunday lunch together. There was also an atmosphere of regret when I would pick up Alisha from her Mum's house. Just a feeling I had which I have been able to detect more acutely since my release from the constrictive relationship I had with Karen.

The date is now the 24th of September 2015 and in the past week I have had the courage to ask Karen if we can talk freely and honestly.

Chapter Four

I am staying in Kathy's cottage in Moelfre, Angelsay as I write this chapter. She is away in America on a music tour with friends, so I am caring for her dog, Clancy, and the cat of no name.

It is a long overdue respite for me after all the trauma of the last few years.

I find the island very spiritual and I am really getting in touch with myself in the solitude of each passing day.

This is an amazing island and I cannot understand why it took me 64 years to get here, but life is like that, I may have missed many other places in the UK. I have attended many AA meeting since my arrival and shared at almost every one but next week I intend to listen in the hope I can receive as well as give.

AA's twelve step program requires of the individual to access true humility and serenity through a process which incorporates the utilisation of all of the steps in sequence. I have come to believe that this is not a program that can picked up and put down for my own convenience. It has to be part of my everyday life as I am so easily distracted by my self-will and the need to people please, thinking that this will find me truth and serenity. Delusional, that's me, a life of fantasy until the consequences are too painful to continue.

I mention this as I have just had to go through a very painful experience culminating in a need to look at my part in the breakup of what I believe to be the only true and meaningful relationship I have ever had. A relationship with my true soul partner. The one with whom I am blessed to have my met on my journey through life.

The realisation that I had lost the one thing that was truly meaningful came through a process of uncomfortable unbalance every time I dropped Alisha off at her Mother's house on a Sunday afternoon. Something was wrong and I felt deeply disturbed each time. It took a year to realise that there was an exchange of what I believe to be pheromones and a spiritual connection when communicating each week. The only way to find out if my beliefs were right was to confront them in God's time with which I was duly presented four weeks before I left for Angelsay.

When I am disturbed I take a look at myself through the program starting with step seven,

'Humbly ask God to remove my shortcomings'.

Shortcomings are evident when I feel disturbed, unhappy, emotionally unbalanced sometimes leading to thoughts of a depressive nature.

Step seven identifies the problem and from there I have to look at my part in the process through a moral inventory in step four. If I find I have been unreasonable, intolerant, dishonest or unfair, then I go to step eight to identify anyone I have harmed. When this is done then direct amends have to be made to those I have harmed unless it is going to hurt them in any way.

I went through this process and was given a God given opportunity to correct my moral inventory when Karen fell ill with her ongoing illness of rheumatic fever.

She really was quite ill and I sent her a bouquet of herbs and heather when I dropped Alisha off on the Sunday afternoon. She texted me later to say she loved them and the caring thoughts that went with them and that she had been in tears to think I still cared. I cried too when the text came through. It was then that I knew she would always be my soul mate even if we were no longer tied by the thin threads of marriage. I have tried so hard to hate her over the past two and a half years but I now knew in my own soul that it is impossible to turn true love into hate even if some say there is a thin line in-between. What they do not realise is that the cross over goes both ways and it is wise to leave the channel open.

Love is blind but it is also indestructible. At least that is what I believe.

We arranged to meet up on neutral ground for an open, honest and free exchange of thoughts and feelings, which we duly did over a fabulous Turkish meal in Morpeth's Ephesus restaurant.

From that night we have agreed to be friends in our own right and not only for the sake of Alisha's peace of mind. From that day the clouds have lifted from my inner self and I feel released from the pressures of resentment, hate and remorse. In consequence I have been able to move on and await the next part of my journey through life.

It is now really exciting to think for the first time in my life I am truly free, but with the knowledge that I have settled down to let love, relationships and freedom from worry take me wherever they want, without the fears that were so exhausting and tied me into a state of mummification.

This is a picture taken off a live broadcast from Rio in Brazil in 2014.

Chapter Four

I am still in Angelsay on my yearly holiday. Two weeks of serenity and a chance to develop further as a human useful being.

I haven't seen much humour in my recent writings and that is sad but it must have been necessary to be serious for a while as I sort my head out.

I started this journey with a visit to Jenni's new house in Hartford, Sheffield. I had delightful time playing with wee Alastair, my grandson. He is growing into a fine Laddie and is learning to swim, ski and do all the things a young lad should do, like playing with a rugby ball, despite the fact his Father is a talented footballer, a complete Tosser, but at least he can think with one part of his body, his feet. He cheated on my daughter the week before Alastair was born and is very lucky that my daughter is a reasonable person and lets him into Alastair's life. Shame the wee lad has his father's name, but what's in a name.

I stayed over-night with them on my way to see Kathy as it is a long haul in my wee car from Northumberland to Angelsay.
The next day I arrived in Angelsay and was warmly welcomed by Kathy, Sion and Clancy the dog.

I was to look after the cottage while Kathy embarked on a trip to New Orleans for the next couple of weeks with a few of her pals.

It wasn't until she had left and I began to settle down that I realised the potential of the next ten days solitude. It has in reflection been a very necessary ingredient of my healing process. In fact it has turned out to be much more than that in respect of my spiritual development.

The Dogs have loved each other's company and has also helped Poppy realise there are other dogs in the world apart from herself. I believe her social skills have improved one hundred percent.

Most of the people I have met here are local to the island area and seem to lean toward a similar category and pattern of motivation. The long term locals, over thirty years roughly are fairly set in their ways and have laid claim to ownership of the cultural format to protect their community.

Understandable as change for them I would imagine is a very scary thought.

The incomers, under thirty years of residence, appear to be sensitive, spiritual runaways from the trials and tribulations of the big bad world in general. At least some of them are artistic in nature, or aspire to be at least, including musicians, thespians and original craft and design such as knitters, woodworkers, blacksmiths and many more but too many to mention. It really is quite tempting to find a category that I might fit into, but I do not think I am ready to hide away quite yet, who knows though?

All that being said I think the island is very beautiful and has future potential for my propensity to "let go and let God". I do not think it is going to be long now until I find the courage to move on to my next phase of development, or adventure. I need to return to Northumberland first to see how I feel about the old familiar surroundings, but I think I detect in my heart that I am not settled or entirely happy in the North East of England.

I feel no personal attachments to my friends where I live at present although they are all lovely people but I do not have any feelings of regret if I leave them behind.

There is a need in my heart for stimulation and need to ask God to show me where he wants me to go next, what he wants me to do with my sobriety and where he wants me to share this precious gift.

"May God's blessing surround me today,
As I trust him and walk in his way,
May his presence within guard and keep me from sin,
To go in peace, joy and love.

20638390R00153

Printed in Great Britain
by Amazon